Be Empowered!

Be Empowered!

Sicilian Mamma's Recipes For Self-Love & Self-Empowerment

Mary Cavaliere

BALBOA.
PRESS
A DIVISION OF HAY HOUSE

Balboa Press books may be ordered through booksellers or by contacting:

Balboa Press
A Division of Hay House
1663 Liberty Drive
Bloomington, IN 47403
www.balboapress.com
1-(877) 407-4847

Printed in the United States of America

ISBN: 978-1-4525-6950-5 (sc)
ISBN: 978-1-4525-6951-2 (e)

Library of Congress Control Number: 2013903587

Balboa Press rev. date: 3/4/2013

Dedication

Everyone in our life has the ability to affect who we are or have become. I could not have become who I am today without participation from the following individuals and the crossing of our paths:

To my lifelong friend, Reverend Linda LaFountain, *who has had unbelievable faith in me and my dream to make a significant contribution to the betterment of the planet. You are one in a million! Ti Amo.*

To my spiritual guru, D'hartma Kravi, *who taught me everything I know about self-love and self-empowerment, and who encouraged me to teach others the same. Without you this book would not have been possible. Namaste.*

To my Mamma, Minnie Theresa Cavaliere, *the little Italian spitfire who always loved me without condition and supported me in living my truth no matter how different it was. Your example taught me how to be strong, and you also taught me how to make the best meatballs on the planet! I love you and I miss you every day.*

To my handsome son, Justin, *the first person in my life who taught me how to love fully without condition...I am so very proud to be your Mamma......I love you.*

To my beautiful daughter, Sammy Jo, *whose unconditional love has been one of the greatest gifts in my life. You are my sunshine Bella...I love you.*

To my best friend, Mary Costa-Jackson, *who set the bar for long-lasting friendship and taught me not settle for anything less. You were my rock! I love you and miss you so very much. Heaven is blessed to have an angel like you.*

To my best friend, Angelo Bell, *who always has my back, and is my brother from another mother. You are not only my paison, you are my family. Ti Amo.*

To my first husband, Bobby, *the catalyst for my spiritual awakening in 1987. It was through you that I found God.*

To my second husband, Robby, *who taught me my grandest lessons in self-empowerment. It was through you that I found myself.*

To Carlos, *my former Life Partner, who blessed me with the gifts of self-validation and acceptance of others. I will see you on the other side for coffee, Sailor. ILYM*

To my sister, Joie, *who has always been more than a sibling....You have been a forever friend. I love you and admire you for all you do for the love of animals.*

To my sister, Toni, *who was always there for me in my time of need, and who loved me unconditionally until the very end. I love you and miss you.*

To my sister, Terri, *the most generous and thoughtful sibling on the planet. Thank you for remaining in my life and loving me unconditionally.*

To my remaining two sisters, Vera, *and* Fran, *who provided me with continual spiritual lessons, which have enabled me to master the priceless gifts of self-love and self-acceptance. I love you both for agreeing to assist.*

Acknowledgements

A heartfelt thank you to **Paul Bacon, Angelo Bell, Karla Bryant, Christine Cimellaro, Lisa Coleman Hasty, Felicia Giouzelis, Lynn Pellerano, Judi Beckwith Swift,** authors **J. Gary Bernhard**, **Michael C. Cordell**, and **Carol Stansfield,** and especially psychologist **Dr. Michael Smith,** for taking the time to assist me with this publication. You all get free Sicilian meatballs for life!

From A Spiritual Master
D'hartma Kravi ~ March 30, 2002

Mary—I want to tell you something. You are a blessed being. You are full of light. Don't forget that. You are greatly enlightened. You have a great deal of honor, understanding, and knowledge. What you do is you walk in my footsteps and you teach people how to love themselves. Most problems occur because people do not remember what self-love and self-empowerment is. They do not even remember they have choices. Tell them. You can do that.

Table of Contents

Recipes For Me, Myself, and I

Recipes For Me, Myself, and Others

Recipes For Me, Myself, and God

Dessert

Recipes For Me, Myself, and I

1

Introductions, Please

I BEGAN MY ACADEMIC JOURNEY LATE in life, at the age of 40. In the spring of 1998, I took a required course in Psychology at Westfield State College. Towards the end of the semester, we were required to present a project on a previously researched topic. Because of prior conversations I had with my professor, she suggested I speak about what I knew best: *self-empowerment.* She also suggested that once the class was over, I hold lectures for other students to offer young people something that could help them at the beginning of their journey called life. Several years later my spiritual guru suggested I teach self-love and self-empowerment. These experiences gave birth to the idea this book is based on.

My personal history was not one of being empowered, but rather one of being controlled. My Sicilian father was so domineering that he did not allow his children to speak at the dinner table. In addition, my sisters and I were not allowed to associate with the opposite sex on any level. When we broke the rules, we were severely punished in ways that were acceptable in the early 1960's, but today would be considered child abuse. One day, my father's reaction to my arriving home late from school, was to swear at me in his native language and throw my books at me. I can also remember being slapped around because I was caught walking with a boy to a school event one evening. On another evening, when my sister and I arrived home late from playing at a friend's house, we were spanked with a wooden spoon and told we were whores. Even when I was a little older, at the age of sixteen, I remember being angry with one of my sisters. I reacted to her behavior by stomping up the stairs to my bedroom. My mother's reaction to my display of emotion was to chase me up the stairs whacking me with a fly swatter, making it entirely clear that showing *my* anger was unacceptable.

I could tell you a dozen more stories like these, some that are even worse, but it would serve no purpose. My point is that my unresolved emotional issues as a child attracted me to situations where I continued to lose my personal power, especially with men. I married not one, but two abusive and unfaithful husbands—the second being worse than the first. The first time my second husband threatened me physically our relationship should have ended. However, my need to be loved and validated by him, as well as by society, was stronger than my need to stand up for myself.

When I was eight months pregnant, my second husband became upset with me for something. His uncontrolled anger caused him to literally pick me up and throw me across the kitchen floor. Up to this point I had never stood up for myself, but because I was pregnant and in fear of losing my child, I became furious. I used that anger, and with the help of the police department, I removed my husband from our home.

My anger is where my journey to becoming self-empowered began, but that is not where it ended. In the days, weeks, months, and years that followed, not only did I learn how to become more empowered, I also learned how to *truly* love myself.

I wrote this book for people who are not leading empowered lives. I wrote it for people who do not have the tools to love themselves, yet desire to make a change, internally and externally. This book is designed to be a quick read, so even the busiest of individuals can fit in a chapter a day. However, I do not want to minimize the amount of effort that must be put forth in order to make changes in ourselves and our lives. It is an ongoing process.

This book is also designed to serve as a reference guide when a coaching reminder is needed. Simply refer to the end of the book for a specific subject matter, and you will be guided back to the chapter or chapters you may need to re-read. Also, at the end of each chapter you are encouraged to take notes on what you read and how it relates to your own life. Where are you in the process? What do you desire to change? My overall mission is to teach others self-love and self-empowerment so they can take control of their lives, and become the liberated and confident individuals they were meant to be.

What I teach goes beyond a psychology textbook. Many of these lessons are born from my experience as a life coach, and most importantly, my own personal experiences. I do not share the intimate details of my journey in order to air my dirty laundry, to place blame on anyone (especially those involved in my stories), or to present myself as a victim. I share the details of my journey to help others understand that transformation can and will occur simply by shifting our perception and behaviors.

Yes, we are a product of our genetic genealogy as well as our environment. My genetics are estimated at 50% Italian and 50% Sicilian which speaks volumes about what I learned as a child with regard to how I should think or behave. Yet, in spite of my upbringing, I have been successful at transforming myself from an emotionally broken, fractured, overly-dramatic, always angry, and sometimes pathetic individual into the strong, self-assured, forgiving, loving, and empowered woman I am today. I believe that if I can accomplish this great feat, so can you.

The lessons in this book can be read and understood in a single day, but they may take days, weeks, months, and sometimes years to actually integrate into your life. Be patient with yourself. You WILL get to your destination! Practice makes perfect, and each day presents an opportunity for transformation. Have faith that YOU control the blueprint for who you would like to become and what you want your life to look like. You deserve to be happy. We all do. So let's get to it!

2

To Thine Own Self Be True

You, yourself, as much as anybody in the entire universe,
deserve love and affection.
~Buddha

One of the most common questions I hear as a life coach is, "How do I love myself?" Here is one way to think about it. When human beings love one another, they show that love by doing whatever they think will make the other person happy. Their actions take on the love they wish to express. When we love others, we show respect, kindness, compassion, and support. Turn these actions inward, and you have *self-love.*

Low self-esteem and low self-worth are at the root of many problems within our society. There are those individuals who use substances such as drugs, alcohol, and food, or activities such as gambling and sex to either numb their inner pain, or to escape from reality on an emotional level. There is also an unhealthy obsession with the lives of celebrities that has consumed our media. Some researchers believe that low self-esteem is the cause of aggression, antisocial behavior, and juvenile delinquency.

Our society has fostered the myth that the more money we

have, the more valuable we are. Relationships feed into our own sense of self-worth, and our emotional shortcomings are expressed through anger, jealousy, and insecurity. Each of these emotions wreaks havoc on our relationships. Again, many are addicted to living vicariously through celebrities, another indication of how we feel about ourselves. Yet those same celebrities are often addicted to drugs, alcohol, and sex because they are unable to fill the void that can only be satisfied by one thing—a love of self.

In order to love yourself, you must do what will make you happy. Sometimes that may not always please others. However, if you make choices based on what others want you to do, although it may satisfy the other person, the feeling that you made the right choice will be temporary. Unfortunately, in the long term, you may not only end up resenting your decision, you may also end up resenting the other individual. The outcome of that choice could result in a broken relationship. Individuals are so busy trying to fill the internal void with other people's love, that they miss out on the greatest love of all—the love of self.

All of this sounds selfish, doesn't it? Well, it is not selfish, and here is the reason why: it is quite common in our personal relationships to give more than we receive. Sooner or later our resentment builds, because the other person is not giving back to us. I am not suggesting you withhold giving to others. It is simply that you must not give from an empty well. If you put yourself first, and make yourself happy, then you will have a "well" that is full enough to be able to give to others completely without expecting anything in return. Loving yourself means being true to yourself at all times.

The following checklist describes ways in which you can show yourself love. Of course this is not a complete list, but it serves as a starting point for you to create your own list:

- ⋆ **Do not accept any kind of abuse from another human being.** Not a spouse, not a parent, not a child, not a sibling, not a peer, and especially not a friend. If you allow someone to abuse you, whether it is physical, verbal, or emotional, you are giving that other individual a free pass to do it again... and again...and again. Allowing yourself to be abused leads to self-hatred and self-loathing, not self-empowerment and self-love.

★ **Be kind and gentle with yourself.** It is important to treat yourself as you would treat others you hold precious and dear. Do not be so hard on yourself. Try being compassionate instead. You are a work in progress. Accept who you are today, no matter how many flaws you have, whether they are character attributes or physical attributes. Always remember this: NO ONE is perfect.

★ **Take care of yourself physically and be cautious about what you put into your body whether it is food, alcohol, or drugs.** Eat consciously and as healthfully as you can. Drink alcohol minimally. Stay away from recreational drugs, as they are an escape from something internal you may need to work on. Take a warm bubble bath with candles, or get a massage when stress sets in. Take a mid-day nap. Participate in a night out with friends. Get plenty of rest.

★ **Take care of yourself emotionally.** Do not allow others to strip you of your personal power through your emotions. Talk to a trusted and supportive friend to work out your negative feelings—whatever they are. Cry until you don't have any tears left. Get into therapy, if that's what you need. Cleanse yourself of any negative emotions you may be harboring. Work on forgiving others to alleviate negative emotions such as anger and resentment.

★ **Maintain physical as well as emotional distance from energy vampires.** You know who these people are. They deplete your energy with all of their personal drama that seems never-ending. It is one thing to be there for a friend or family member. It is another to have them suck the life right out of you. Do not be afraid to draw boundaries and minimize your contact with these individuals.

* **Take care of yourself spiritually by taking time out to connect with God, The Universe, or whomever or whatever you feel is your higher power.** Spend time with nature. Listen to music. Go to church. Meditate. Breathe. Pray. Write. Reflect. Always know you are a child of a most loving energy (sometimes called God).

* **If you are broke, do not lend anyone else money.** If you're physically exhausted, do not agree to remodel your best friend's living room. If you're emotionally bankrupt, do not try to save your sister's marriage. Work on filling up your own well. Then when you give, you will do so from a state of abundance rather than a place of lack.

* **Give yourself permission to say "No" to others.** Give yourself permission to change your mind when something is not working for you. Give yourself permission to feel whatever you need to feel in the moment. Give yourself permission to not feel guilty about taking care of YOU.

* **Stop care-taking.** I'm not referring to your children or your elderly parents. I'm referring to a toxic relationship with people who have an addiction. Whether they are abusing drugs, alcohol, gambling, shopping, or sex, it is not up to you to take care of them or fix them. In fact, if you consistently rescue them, then they have no reason to change. This is also known as enabling or co-dependency. At the base of co-dependency is the need to feel good about yourself through being needed by someone else. This is not how you build authentic self-esteem or self-worth. Encourage the other

person to seek help, and if they refuse, you may need to consider ending your relationship with him or her.

* **Celebrate your ethnicity.** Know where you came from, and be proud of your heritage. Do not allow anyone to belittle you or insult you or discredit you based on your ancestry. In today's world, it is no longer acceptable.

Learning how to love and respect myself was one of the hardest things to integrate into my life because of my cultural background. When you grow up in a Sicilian-Italian environment, you learn to feel guilty about everything. In 1980, I was so unhappy in my life that I sought therapy. I was fortunate enough to find a woman who was Jewish, so she completely understood the environment of guilt in which I had been raised. I will never forget her name because she helped me to eliminate guilt from my emotional repertoire. How liberating it was to make choices based on respecting myself and my own feelings! I did learn, however, there was still much more work to do in order to love myself fully.

I allowed myself to be abused by more than one man in my life. It started in high school with my very first boyfriend and led to two marriages that were physically and emotionally abusive. In both marriages, when my husbands cheated, I took partial responsibility for their affairs, and allowed both men to return only to hurt me further with more infidelity. I made this choice because I did not value myself enough to say goodbye the first time I was made aware of the cheating. Have you ever asked a woman who is being abused why she stays? The most common answer is, "Because I love him." I now know that enduring abuse in any form is NOT love. *I didn't stay because I loved them. I stayed because I didn't love me.* The good news is that these experiences enabled me to master self-love and self-empowerment. I have had several relationships since my second divorce, but none that encompassed abuse or infidelity. I began to attract different types of men, because I had finally mastered the lesson of not allowing abuse.

What I have also come to learn is that the more you love yourself, the more others will respect and love you as well. It works like a magnet. If there are people in your life that do not love you because you choose to love yourself, you may need to distance yourself from them. This distance will allow you to continue to grow and flourish, while simultaneously providing them with a lesson for their own growth.

Loving yourself goes hand in hand with self-empowerment, which is why all of the other lessons in this book speak just as much to loving oneself as they do to becoming more empowered.

Shakespeare wrote, in "Hamlet," *"THIS ABOVE ALL, TO THINE OWN SELF BE TRUE."* Live by these words and your life will change forever.

Ways In Which I Do Not Love Myself

Ways In Which I Will Show Myself Love

3

THE POWER OF CHOICE

The strongest principle of growth lies in the human choice.
~George Eliot

ONE OF THE MOST IMPORTANT elements to becoming self-empowered is the understanding that we always have choices, and that those choices do not have to be associated with right or wrong.

We have the right to choose our thoughts, feelings, and behavior. We have the right to choose what to do with our time and our life. We also have the right to choose what we do *not* want to do with our time and our life. We all have access to "free will." For this reason, it's important to eliminate the word "should" from your vocabulary. There are no "shoulds." There is only choice—your choice. The caveat in making your choices is that you must own those choices and also take responsibility for them.

Freedom of choice does not translate to having NO boundaries, or doing whatever you want whenever you want with whomever you want, although ultimately you do have that choice. If you're having an argument with your spouse, you might have the temptation to hit them over the head with a frying pan. For me to imply that harming another human being is an acceptable choice would be irresponsible on my part. Using the freedom of choice effectively in life means having very clear boundaries that are based on your personal value system, and refining your choices based on those values while remaining within the boundaries of the law and human kindness.

An example might be making the choice to become involved romantically with someone who is married. You can certainly be empowered and make that choice, but if you feel it was inappropriate for your own spouse to cheat on you, then this choice will not resonate with your personal value system. You will know when you have crossed the line, even if you're not willing to admit it to anyone else. You may end up feeling ashamed rather than empowered, and as a result you will keep your actions private to avoid being judged.

It is challenging to take responsibility for everything you do, say, think, and feel. To do so is key, however, as it allows you to have complete control of your life once you learn how to master it. Individuals do not always take responsibility for what they do, mainly because it is much easier to blame someone else for everything that is going wrong in their life. Blaming others is the most impulsive reaction you may have to your life challenges, but the unfortunate part is that blaming doesn't lead you anywhere constructive. It leads you to think of yourself as a victim, which is the extreme opposite of being empowered.

You must also take responsibility for what you say. You have opinions and viewpoints, but when and how you share your viewpoint can have an enormous impact on your relationships. If you're going to say something in the name of honesty that you know is going to hurt someone, you will need to take responsibility for the outcome of your choice. If you are comfortable with that possible outcome, then go for it. If you are not, think of a more compassionate way of saying what you feel you need to say. If you're Sicilian like me, and sometimes have trouble filtering what rolls off the tip of your tongue, become aware of your behavior, take responsibility for it, and if you care deeply about the relationship you have with the other person, apologize for it.

Although you are entitled to your feelings, whatever they may be, you must also realize you are responsible for how you express those feelings, as well as for the way in which you choose to react to what others do or say. If someone hurts you, or you experience loss, you are responsible for how you react, whether positive or negative. This sort of thinking is foreign to most of us and therefore requires a great deal of work on our part to be able to transform pain into something positive rather than negative.

A great example would be if someone you were seeing for the last year decided to break up with you. A negative reaction would be hanging onto the pain and remaining angry and depressed for an unreasonable period of time, putting up walls to shut out others that could have the potential to hurt you, obsessing about the other person's life after the break-up, or making the decision to seek revenge on your former lover for rejecting you in the first place. A positive reaction would be to recognize this person was not the right one for you, taking some time to heal your wounds, re-building your confidence, and then moving forward and being open to love with someone else in the future.

Each of us is responsible for our own perceptions and attitudes. I am not suggesting you should not feel, but it is important to realize that your thought process can be the real cause of continual pain and suffering over something that may have happened a week ago, a month ago, or years ago. That suffering is connected to your views, opinions, biases, judgments, and your personal outlook on life. If you are able to shift what you think, you can shift your pain or negative feelings as well. You have a choice every day between being a victim, and being empowered. Your primary goal is to choose the positive over the negative. A negative choice will either keep you stagnant or move you backward, where a positive choice will always move you forward.

Saying "No" is one of the hardest things for human beings to do because no one wants to disappoint others. Nevertheless, keep in mind that being a people-pleaser is often at your own expense. This does not mean you should never compromise, or that you should always get your way in matters that involve other people, but what you can do instead, is choose your battles wisely. When something is really important to you, do not say yes when you want to say no. If you do, you may begin to feel resentful while you're doing it, and you will make yourself miserable. Either way, going against your own feelings serves no one. You deserve to be happy, not miserable, so sometimes you may need to say "No" to avoid the self-inflicted misery caused by saying "Yes." Be kind to yourself and love yourself enough to say "No."

It is also perfectly acceptable to say, "I've changed my mind." Say it as nicely as you can, but don't be afraid to say it. "I really appreciate it, but I'm going to have to pass" or "I apologize if I've inconvenienced you, but I've changed my mind" or "I'm so sorry, but I've had a change of heart." These will all work just fine. The key is to decline when that is truly what you want to do. You do not have to make excuses or defend your position. In fact, defending yourself implies guilt on your part. Making choices that serve you and your happiness should not translate to guilt, because guilt will erode your self-esteem.

There are times when it may be difficult to make a choice at all. In these situations what you can do is follow through each scenario, either in your head or on paper, until you can determine what the worst-case scenario will be. Facing the worst and realizing it is not as bad as you originally thought may help you to determine your destination. It also allows you to create a Plan B in your mind that will minimize the fear of Plan A not working out as you had hoped. You can also sit quietly and ask yourself this question: "What would be the most empowering action I can take in this situation?" Think this question through, and make a written list of all the possible repercussions of your choices. In this way you can make a well-thought out decision that you feel comfortable with.

One of my harshest lessons in life was my second marriage. More than one person warned me about the man I was about to marry. I knew he had cheated on his first wife, and I also knew he had been abusive to her. Here is what I told myself: "Oh, he was just unhappy with her...he would never do that to me...he loves me more than he ever loved her!" Even though I had seen red flags during our courtship with both of these issues, I ignored them and married him anyway. Ten years later, after two incidents of infidelity (and I'm sure there were others I did not know about), and a marriage filled with physical abuse, I finally divorced him.

Today, we have an amicable relationship. We have no problem being in the same room bantering with one another, which we both seem to enjoy. When I moved to California, he was going through a rough time, so I offered him items from my home to get him re-established. When he is behind on his child support I work with him to resolve the issue instead of bringing him to court to battle over the arrearage. Others have asked me how I can be so kind to him, or how I can even be in the same room with him, after all he put me through. I do understand why others question my behavior, but what I also understand is that I was the one who made the choice to marry him. I was the one who made the choice to stay with him after he cheated the first time. I was the one who made the choice to remain in spite of the abuse. I could play the victim in this situation. That would be the easy choice. The more challenging choice, and one I feel better about, was to forgive him and to understand and accept that I contributed to the drama that unfolded between us. I made a poor choice, and I paid dearly for that choice. Not only should I have divorced him long before I actually did, but I never should have married him in the first place. Yet that marriage, for me, was the springboard for mastering self-empowerment and self-love. That is the reason why I no longer hold resentment, but instead, feel grateful for the experience.

Remember, your personal power lies in your choices. As you continue to grow and evolve, your choices will evolve as well. As Maya Angelou says, "When we know better, we do better."

Ways In Which I Make Destructive Choices

Ways In Which I Can Make Constructive Choices

4

Moment To Moment

If you spend your whole life waiting for the storm.....
you'll never enjoy the sunshine.
~Morris West

PART OF AN ACTOR'S TRAINING is to live in the moment. What exactly is living in the moment? Buddhists label it as being "mindful." Being mindful is paying close attention, observing closely.

The reason this is key in an actor's work, is that if you just say the lines the way you think they should be said, based on your interpretation of the character, then that is what your performance consists of—you saying the lines based on your interpretation of the character—which results in a shallow performance. Actors use living in the moment as their tool. It allows them to think and feel what the character would be thinking and feeling at that moment in time. By living in the moment of the character, the actor creates reality for the audience. This makes an actor's performance organic and authentic, as well as fulfilling for both the actor and the audience.

This same concept can be applied to real life. Using walking as an example, being mindful results in not being distracted by thoughts of your to-do list at home, but, rather, allows you to take in the fresh air, the sunshine, the clouds, and the trees. In order to live in the moment, you cannot allow your mind to become preoccupied with anything else other than what is right in front of you.

Mindfulness is currently being used in psychology as treatment for depression, anxiety, drug-addiction relapse, and obsessive-compulsive disorder. This type of focus allows you to make a shift in the thoughts, feelings, and even bodily sensations that contribute to your emotional instability. The reason mindfulness works, is that the mind can only give attention to one thing at a time, so if your focus is on a positive, it cannot be on a negative. Mindfulness, when used while eating, is extremely beneficial as well. The sensation of fullness does not come from your stomach, but from your brain. Dieticians and fitness experts say that it takes 15-20 minutes for your body to notify the brain that your stomach is full. Therefore, the slower you eat, the less food it will take to feel full. As a result you will eat less, and therefore lose weight.

When you choose to live in the past or the future, you lose the present moment because you are elsewhere. Living in the past is futile, because you have already lived that moment and it is gone from you forever. Should you learn from your past? Absolutely. Should you hold onto fond memories? Of course. Do you need to dwell on the past, especially a negative past? Definitely not. Do you need to think about the future? In order to meet your goals and objectives in life, you do have to give the future some consideration. Do you need to dwell on the future? No, you do not. Dwelling can cause you to worry or be concerned, and again, you will lose out on the present moment. Worry is such a useless waste of your energy. No matter how much you focus on worrying, it will not change the outcome of your future or any given situation.

Living in the moment will allow you to enjoy everyday activities more fully. Bathing your child can sometimes be a chore, but it can also be fun if you're playful with your child during the process. Grocery shopping may feel like a task, but it can also be enjoyable if you engage in the creative process involved in meal planning and making dinner for your loved ones. Or you can challenge yourself to see how much money you can save by using coupons or becoming a comparative shopper. Getting on a treadmill might be something you dread, but rather than focusing on how long you have to exercise, pop a movie into your DVD to enjoy the time you are on the treadmill, all while catching up on films you may have missed in the theater.

Now that you are beginning to see the pattern, let's move on to something bigger. Most of us tend to fantasize about the grass being greener on the other side of the fence, so we run through life searching for the "right place to live", the "right job to have" or "the right partner to love." The problem with that approach is that sooner or later we will find some flaw in that place, that job, or that partner, and thus the perpetual search continues. Because we are always en route, we never arrive at our destination.

Acceptance of where you are currently at is a powerful tool to help you to live in the moment. An attitude of gratitude can go a long way in transforming your state of mind. If you are not happy about the job you are in, you must strive to find acceptance of where you are currently at, and be grateful for the positive things you are experiencing in that job until a different job can be secured.

If you are not happy about being alone, and not having someone to share your life with, you must look for the positive aspects of being alone. These might include such things as being able to make plans with others spontaneously, without having to include or consider anyone else or, choosing not to do the laundry or dishes for a week simply because you don't feel like it. Being alone could also mean not having to share the television remote—or staying in bed until two in the afternoon. There are many ways in which you can feel grateful for being alone.

If you are feeling unhappy about something that has happened in the past, a situation in which someone hurt you or betrayed you, for example, you can look for a lesson in that experience which will transform the negative experience into a positive one. Then you can let the negativity of that experience go and move on in the present moment.

We can learn a great deal from children and animals as both find it quite natural to live in the moment. A toddler and a puppy only care about what they are experiencing at the current moment in time. They have not focused on the past or the future, which allows their spirit to be free. In essence, you need to free yourself by recognizing that YOU are where the party is. "Party" is just a metaphor for finding the joy in the present moment right before you.

Being mindful and living in the moment takes a great deal of practice to master, especially in an age where we are so distracted by technology as well as other things vying for our attention. However, the benefits are worth it. Not only will you find more inner peace and happiness, but the physical benefits also make it worth the effort. Psychologists and physicians both say that living fully in the moment reduces stress, boosts your immune system, reduces chronic pain, lowers blood pressure, and even reduces heart disease.

My greatest lesson in living in the moment came late in my life. I became so focused on making a career change that I thought was for the better, that I lost sight of enjoying the present. Focusing on the future in an obsessive way not only had a severe impact on my health, but it also destroyed my happiness for a brief period. When my health immobilized me, I was forced to turn within to analyze how I had become so broken. In essence, I needed to accept where I was. I needed to focus on the moment and enjoy things as they were, rather than focusing on what was to become. Although I was not in the job I wanted to be in, I did not live in the place I wanted to live, and I was not doing all the things I loved to do, I managed to make the most of where I was at and enjoy what was in front of me. I had a stable job with good money and benefits. I was surrounded by people who loved me and friends who treated me like family. I continued to do the things I loved on a part-time basis, and that is what kept me going and allowed me to remain positive and happy in my life, even though it was not perfect.

Live in the present moment and approach life with as much mindfulness as you can muster. No matter what is going on in your life, there are always positives in every situation. As corny as it sounds, all you need to do is search for the silver lining in the clouds. You will find it. You simply need to be willing to look hard enough.

Things I Am Grateful For In My Life

Ways In Which I Can Be More Mindful

5

THE TIDES OF CHANGE

Resisting change is as futile as resisting the weather.
~Warren Bennis

IN 1998, I READ *WHO Moved My Cheese?* by Spencer Johnson. It was one of the best books I had ever read. In a very humorous way, using two mice who are looking for cheese, the author makes several key points which include (1) change always happens, so we must anticipate it, (2) we must adapt to it quickly, and (3) we should try to enjoy it.

The company I worked for at that time jumped on the bandwagon to create workshops around the Who-Moved-My-Cheese philosophy. As a result, the book received some criticism that it was being used to try and convince employees that their unhappiness at work was relative to their inability to accept company reorganizations, cost-cutting measures, or down-sizing. I can certainly understand why people felt that way, but I did not see the workshops as a misuse of the book.

The reality is that things change. Sometimes good things come to an end. This is an inevitable part of life. The sooner you can accept change and move forward, the more empowered you will become.

I recognize that there are people who find it easy to embrace change, and there are people who find it challenging to embrace change. It doesn't matter which side of the fence you are on, because change does not discriminate and you will experience it whether you want to or not. One of the best approaches to accepting change is to turn the negative into something positive by using the opportunity to learn and grow. It will be a less painful experience if you choose to view change in this way. Not accepting the change does not mean it will reverse itself. It will move forward like a steamroller over your desires and wishes, and either way you will end up on the other side of the change. To accept it and view it as a positive means it will still occur, but you will experience less discomfort and suffering.

Sometimes faith plays a huge role in accepting change. If you are able to let go and turn your life over to your higher power, the transition will be easier. Whether you are trying to accept the ending of a relationship or the loss of a job, your trust in your higher power is a powerful tool, if you choose to use it. The beautiful part about change is that in the future when you are able to look back on the experience, you will realize that the change was for the better even though it felt negative at the time. Comfort can be found in knowing that hindsight will allow you the ability to find the positive that can come out of change.

Loss of any kind is never easy. I myself have gone through an enormous amount of loss throughout my life. My father, my mother, my sister, and my best friend all passed away sooner than expected. I went through not one but two devastating divorces. They say what doesn't kill you makes you stronger, and I have to admit that this is true. Although I never want to be faced with loss again, I know I will process it differently now than I did ten years ago because I understand it is a process, and I choose to move through it as quickly as I can. This does not mean I stop missing those who have passed over. It just means I am able to accept the loss and move on with life with as little discomfort as possible.

According to the Kubler-Ross model of grief, there are the five emotional phases one must go through, whether we have lost a spouse, a parent, a sibling, a friend, a pet, or a job:

Phase 1 is **DENIAL,** when we do not want to believe what is happening to us. Obviously, if we are dealing with a death, we move through this phase fairly quickly, but if we're dealing with an impending divorce, we can remain stuck in this phase for a very long period of time.

Phase 2 is **ANGER** , when we question "Why me?" It is the phase where most people blame others or God for their pain and suffering.

Phase 3 is **BARGAINING,** when we try to maintain the status quo by either praying to God, or telling the other person involved that we will do anything not to lose him or her. It is our desire to postpone or delay the discomfort of the change.

Phase 4 is **DEPRESSION**, when a full understanding is present of what is about to occur or has already occurred. It is a feeling of hopelessness as well as a time of crying and grieving. It is a normal and extremely important part of the process, and should not be avoided. It is also the most common phase that immobilizes people, and this is why it is critical to keep moving forward and persevering through it.

Phase 5 is **ACCEPTANCE**, when we finally understand that everything is going to be okay and we come to terms with the change.

About a year after I moved to California, I endured a change that I never ever expected. I have always been able to take care of myself and my children financially. Money was never an issue for me because from the time I graduated high school, I was diligent in my efforts to be successful. My family was poor and I was determined to not live the same way as an adult. Even without a college education, I had a successful career in Information Technology, which allowed me to buy nice things, live wherever I wanted, and to even own my own home without the help of a spouse. That is what I had always been accustomed to.

But as a newcomer to California, I was terminated from a job for the first time in my life, at the worst possible time, while I was in the middle of purchasing a home with my sister. Had I been purchasing the home on my own, I would have stopped the sale until I secured new income, but my sister had just sold the entire contents of her home on the east coast, and driven across the country with all of her animals in tow. At the time, I didn't see a way out of the situation. Against my better judgment, I went through with the sale.

Although I eventually secured employment, it was at a salary that was $15,000 less per year than the job I had just been let go from. To complicate matters further, we discovered after moving into the house, that the real estate agent we had used had not been completely honest with us about what the monthly mortgage would be. I tried everything I could to keep up with the payments, but I now found myself in a financial situation to which I was unaccustomed. To make a long story short, I ended up turning the deed to the house over to my sister who sold it, took the majority of the profit we had made in the year we lived together, and purchased another, less costly home for herself. My decision to let go of the house caused an enormous discord in my relationship with my sister, because she felt I had abandoned her. She stopped speaking to me for the next three years. I was forced into filing bankruptcy, which was extremely uncomfortable for someone who had always been able to handle her finances with integrity. I was devastated because I lost my home, my sister, my higher income, and my credit.

So along came *denial*. I couldn't believe this was happening to me—someone who had always been able to take care of herself in such a comfortable fashion. It didn't take long to move into the *anger* phase. Why me? I felt as if God was punishing me for something. All of the spiritual training I had went right out the window. I became furious with God and therefore, made a conscious choice to walk away from my spiritual evolution. What came next was *bargaining.* I got on my knees and told God if he helped me out of this mess I would never walk away from him again. I couldn't stand the discomfort of my situation any longer. There were weeks where I only had fifty dollars for groceries for my daughter and myself. I can even remember one day when I had to ask my boss to work from home because I didn't have any money for gas to get there, and the office was only seven miles away. It was an extremely humiliating and humbling phase in my life. All of this of course brought on the *depression.* Where had I gone wrong? How was I ever going to get out of this mess? I remained in the depression phase, living off of payday loans, for at least two years.

On my 50th birthday, a former boss and friend of mine sent me *The Secret*, a film documentary that was released in 2006 along with the book by Rhonda Byrne. *The Secret* teaches us that everything we want or need can be manifested through the power of the mind and maintaining a positive emotional state.

I was already familiar with the concepts of *The Secret* because I had learned these concepts many years ago from my own spiritual guru long before this publication hit the bookshelves. Having the video allowed me to watch it over and over again, which reinforced what I already knew. This is when things turned around for me. I had finally made it to the *acceptance* phase.

Retrospection has allowed me to see everything that happened in a positive light, so I have become grateful for the experience. First, I learned how to make a budget and live by it, something I had never done in my adult life. Second, I learned how to live within my means using mainly my cash income, and only tapping into credit during emergencies. Third, I learned how to save money by only buying items that are on sale, which stretched my dollars to their maximum. The most important lesson I learned, however, was that I am not how much money I have or what I own, but who I am as a person. This part of my learning is what transformed me into a minimalist. Even though I went on to make over $25,000 more per year than when I lost my job, the lessons I have learned remained. I continue to follow a budget, stretch my dollars as far as I can, live mainly from cash income, and only buy items that are on sale.

Give yourself time to adapt to change. No one is immediately comfortable with it. How you handle change, and especially how you handle loss, is up to you. You can surrender to the change and accept what you cannot control, or you can resist it and dwell on it for the next ten years of your life. It is up to you whether you want to learn and grow, or whether you want to enter the world of emotional stagnation. All events in your life are temporary. If you are open to it, time does heal all wounds.

Ways In Which I Resist Change

Things I Would Like To Change In My Life

6

The Man In The Mirror

It is easier to fight for one's principles than to live up to them.
~Alfred Adler

All of us possess values that define our character and guide us in determining what is meaningful to us. These values are usually inherited from our parents or teachers. My Sicilian roots were indirectly connected to the mafia. Had my parents or my siblings chose these same values, our lives would have looked completely different. As adults we can determine the personal, spiritual, or family values we want to live by. Recognizing that this is easier said than done, these insights will hopefully help you to stand strong for what resonates for you.

When you have to work hard to justify or validate your values to others, you are giving your power away to those individuals. There is nothing to validate. There is nothing to justify. Your values are just that—*your* values. You own them. Or at least you should. Part of being an adult is making choices that work for you. So if you own values that are only based on what your parents think, or what others think, then you are not living an authentic life that brings you happiness. Your parents can certainly guide you when you are young to choose values they believe will transform you into a responsible adult who contributes to society. As you age, you may come to realize those values no longer serve you in the way you would like them to.

Beyond the challenge of justifying your chosen values to your family, you are constantly inundated with messages from the current political and religious factions, many of which are trying to push their own values on others. The ongoing political and spiritual war in our country is frustrating for everyone. It would be in our best interest if everyone could allow others the simple right to live their lives in a way that makes them happy. Period.

The question then is, why are people trying so hard to push their opinions on others? I believe it is so they can prove they are right and others are wrong. Why are people judging others so harshly? In a nutshell, judgment allows us to feel superior to others. If we can somehow label what another does as "wrong," then we can justify elevating ourselves to feel better. There is only one problem with this logic. It does not serve us in a way that benefits ourselves or others.

As I indicated in a previous chapter, ultimately there is no right or wrong. There is only choice—your choice and their choice. You need to stand by your own choices. If you engage with others who cannot respect those choices, then you may need to distance yourselves from those individuals in order to be who you want to be. You also must recognize that if you want others to honor and respect your choices, then you also need to honor and respect their choices as well.

Gay marriage is certainly a topic where spiritual values conflict on a grand scale. We are told by one group, who follow a specific spiritual doctrine, it is "wrong" for two individuals of the same sex to be married. Yet on the other side, we hear that because our Constitution was created to allow equal rights for all, it is "wrong" for two individuals who love each other to not have the same rights as everyone else. Who is right and who is wrong? Both positions are based on value systems, but when those value systems impact laws that affect others who do not possess the same values we do, we enter into dangerous territory. What I encourage instead is for you to feel good about yourself in a way that does not include judging another's choices or path.

If a woman chooses to be a stripper for a living, who are we to judge? Are we God? Can we find any spiritual doctrine that endorses our right to judge? I don't think we can. Would I make the choice to be a stripper myself? Probably not, because I do not feel that career path would allow me to feel empowered. However, that does not give me the right to impose my personal value system on the woman who enjoys this line of work, or feels the need to do this sort of work to meet her financial obligations.

My spiritual belief is that love on any level cannot be wrong, so I am an advocate of gay marriage. However, for the purposes of argument, suppose I did not support gay marriage. Do I have the right to take that privilege away from anyone else? No, I do not. The only right I should have is the choice to marry or not marry a woman myself, if that were part of my value system.

By all means be empowered and honor your values with conviction, but only do this *for yourself.* Pushing your agenda on someone else who may not be comfortable with your choice is an indication of your own inability to connect with others in a more meaningful way. If you are judgmental and critical, whether based on your personal values or not, I can assure you that your relationships will fail as a result. I am attempting to provide you with an opportunity to enhance your relationships by letting go of judgment and allowing others their own truth.

In a situation where you don't agree with someone, the best possible outcome would be to agree to disagree, which indicates that you appreciate the other individual's position, but simply do not agree in a respectful way. This is not always easy to do. In fact, I myself have not yet mastered this incredibly challenging concept, although I do feel I'm further along than the average person. Have you ever met an Italian or Sicilian who was not opinionated or judgmental? If you have, please introduce them to me. I want to study them closer and learn from them.

Judgment is a learned behavior that I myself am still working on eliminating from my psychological repertoire. So I will offer this tool that I am currently using. If you truly cannot accept the value system of another, at minimum do not judge, do not criticize, and do not express to that person that he or she is wrong and you are right. Simply walk away in peace and allow that person to be who he or she chooses to be.

A woman I used to know was guilty of constantly assessing the actions of others. She repeatedly judged in a way that was annoying to everyone around her. I don't think I ever spent time with her without hearing her say "That's wrong" or "That isn't right" about something or someone. Her perpetual judgment of others was, at times, infuriating. Her negative behavior left her with few close friends, and impacted her children who grew up with very little self-esteem. Although I recognize that her own lack of accomplishment might have been at the root of her severe judgment of others, my point would be to ask you this. Who wants to be around this type of individual? Criticism of others could result in repelling people you truly desire to have in your life.

Because I am an ordained minister, I am repeatedly confronted with the value systems of others. People judge me for swearing or getting angry because they believe that, as a member of the clergy, I should be "angelic" at all times. This is their way of trying to pigeonhole me into following their personal value system instead of allowing me my own truth. I could name several members of the clergy that I myself do not see as angelic or perfect, but I won't. Ordained I am. Human I am. Sicilian I am. Perfect I am not.

So what is it that makes people feel good about themselves? How does someone increase his or her feelings of self-esteem? Some do it by building on their accomplishments and being proud of who they are. Then there are others that try to feel better about themselves by putting others down. Stop and think the next time you are criticizing someone and ask yourself why you are doing it. You may find it has more to do with how you are feeling about yourself. The more self-love and self-esteem you have, the more you will be able to see great things in others.

Jesus had it right when he said "Why do you look at the speck of sawdust in your brother's eye and pay no attention to the plank in your own eye?" Analyzing other people's lives and actions is a waste of your time and energy. Instead use that energy in a more positive way by looking at yourself in the mirror, and analyze your own life, your own value systems, and work to make changes to be the best person you can be. The only thing this can possibly lead to is a higher sense of self-esteem.

My Personal Values

Ways In Which I Judge Others Harshly

7

K.I.S.S.

The more you have, the more you are occupied, the less you give.
But the less you have, the more free you are.
~Mother Teresa

MAYBE YOU'VE HEARD IT BEFORE, and maybe you haven't. K.I.S.S. is an acronym for KEEP IT SIMPLE STUPID. One of the ways to embrace self-empowerment is to learn how to live a simpler life, which is characterized by satisfaction with what we need rather than what we want.

We work our tails to the bone to acquire "stuff" because having great "stuff" makes us feel good about ourselves, and here is why. It communicates to others who we are. It tells others we have money (even if we don't). It tells others we are in a different class than they are (a better one). It tells others we are a success story or that we are superior. The downside of owning expensive or excessive "stuff" is that it only makes us feel good about ourselves temporarily.

A mindset stuck in materialism is a mindset that is not growing. The question you must always ask yourself is "If I lost all of my material possessions, then who would I be? What will then define me as a human being?" Personal possessions do not define who you are. Your heart and your mind define who you are along with your intentions and personal values. If you are putting forth a façade, pretending to afford things you really cannot afford, you are adding unnecessary financial stress to your life, not to mention you are living a lie, which also adds to your stress. You can and will exhaust yourself by always trying to outdo others.

How much make-up will help you to feel more attractive? How many pairs of shoes will satisfy your need to feel sexy? How many designer labels will improve your self-worth? How much do you need to spend on a car to impress everyone else? If you are not feeling very good about yourself on the inside, then you will have an insatiable need for these types of things on the outside in an attempt to self-validate.

Obviously, if you can afford these items in excess, there is nothing wrong with buying them, although you may still want to reflect on why you feel the need to go to such extremes. However, if you cannot afford them, and you are placing yourself in debt to acquire them, this is an indication that you are out of balance, and this imbalance needs to be addressed. Also keep in mind you may still be out of balance even if you can afford an abundance of "things".

Some celebrities are perfect examples of emotional and spiritual imbalances. We have witnessed over and over again how having money and fame does not satisfy emotional or psychological needs through the lives (and deaths) of Marilyn Monroe, Elvis Presley, Janice Joplin, Michael Jackson, Amy Winehouse, and most recently, Whitney Houston. They were all living the dream that many of us would love to attain, yet they were still unhappy tortured souls for whom no amount of material possessions or validation from others was ever enough. They felt the need to indulge in drugs, alcohol, and destructive behaviors to numb their pain and escape the gaping hole in their souls. It is a very sad and powerful imbalance to watch.

If you really want to self-validate, you should try spending less on material possessions you don't need and use that money to help someone who is in need. Watch as it transforms who you are and how you feel about yourself. There are so many more useful and rewarding things you could do with your money if you didn't spend so much of it trying to prove to others your value and worth.

Now, let's talk about clutter. Clutter = Confusion, Chaos, and Disorder. Clutter in your environment is a reflection of the clutter in your mind or with your emotions. In order to attain more clarity in your life and feel more empowered, you must remove the chaos and the confusion, which means removing the clutter. This has become such a common problem in our society that we now have television shows dedicated to compulsive shopping, clutter, and hoarding, not to mention professional organizers.

Take a look at the inside of your car and the inside of your home. These are a reflection of who you are and where you are. Often, clutter and disorganization are symptoms of a bigger problem. If you are suffering from an emotional trauma, grief, or have been diagnosed with attention deficit disorder or chronic depression, you may find it challenging to get organized. If you feel it is too daunting of a task to do it yourself, then ask a friend who is organized to help you, or even hire a professional. There is plenty of free information out on the Internet on de-cluttering and getting organized, so take full advantage of it.

If you suspect you are a hoarder, which means your clutter has taken over your living, dining, and sleeping spaces, your quality of life is suffering substantially. This is an extreme condition that requires assistance from a mental health professional.

I have said this a thousand times to myself: "If I had saved every dollar I have spent on wasteful things over the last thirty years that I later gave away or threw away, I could have retired at the age of forty." I recognize the reason I was so frivolous with my money was that I had a solid income, which allowed me to squander it whenever I felt the need. Having always been a financially independent and successful woman, I thought there would be an endless supply of money. However, later in life, as I noted earlier, I experienced a traumatic financial hardship that caused me to take stock of how much I disrespected money, and the ways in which I was continuing to spend it in a destructive way. That experience allowed me to change forever, and the byproduct was my evolution into what is known as minimalism. I own only what is necessary for my basic comfort, and I stretch my dollars as far as they can go by either purchasing something used or buying it new on sale. This is one of the ways I feel more empowered as I live my life with more purpose and a positive intent. I also feel grateful to have arrived at this liberating state of mind.

Every six months to a year I go through everything I own and if I haven't used it or worn it in the last year or so, it goes. When I was a young girl our Italian Mamma taught us to give things we didn't need away to others less fortunate than ourselves. I have always followed that philosophy throughout most of my life. Even now, if I own something that is in excellent condition, and I can think of someone who might want or need it, I offer it to him or her free of charge prior to listing it on Craig's List or bringing it to Goodwill.

It can be overwhelming to reduce the amount of "stuff" you own. Do not try and do it all at once. Take a room at a time, or even a dresser or a closet at a time, and begin the process of cleaning out the clutter. Sell a few things, and take the cash and reward yourself with a long weekend away, a day at the spa, or put it into a bank account to build your savings. Better yet, put it toward paying down a debt.

Donate a few things to charity, and don't forget to get a receipt to deduct the donation on your taxes. Once you have things organized, everything you own should be stored in its designated space and should be returned to that place when not in use.

You will be amazed at how empowered you will feel when the chaos in your life is eliminated. You will feel uplifted, less congested, and you will experience more joy because simplicity truly is one of life's greatest treasures.

Areas In My Home To De-Clutter

Items To Sell Or Donate

8

To Dream The Impossible Dream

When I was a child my mother said to me, "If you become a soldier, you'll be a general. If you become a monk, you'll be the pope." Instead I became a painter and wound up as Picasso."
~Pablo Picasso

I HAVE ALWAYS FOUND IT A bit odd, as well as sad, that some people either do not possess an innate urge to do something they are passionate about, or that they have this inner urging, but choose to ignore it. Having a dream and working towards that dream can be one of the most fulfilling aspects of our lives.

We hear testimony all the time from individuals who have reached their dreams as entertainers, writers, sports figures, and business leaders. It is foolish to think they arrived where they are overnight, although there are a select few that have experienced success in this manner. The majority, however, probably dedicated many years of hard work, experienced an enormous amount of rejection, exhibited perseverance, and possessed a solid belief in themselves to bring their dream to fruition.

Many times dreams are left untouched because of fear of failure. Yet inside there is still a burning passion to pursue something that speaks to one's soul. Whatever the dream is, it is not only important to you, but possibly to everyone else on the planet as well. Why? Because those who are living their dream have a profound impact on those who are not. They are inspirational and show others that obstacles can be overcome, and we can all reach our destination.

Oprah once said, "One thing I do know for sure is if you don't follow your dreams, it will destroy you." She is so right. It is so important to follow your dream. What if your dream does not seem practical? The worst-case scenario is that you might have to alter it a bit based on physical or financial limitations, or you may have to pursue your dream part-time while you do something else, but that is perfectly acceptable. What is most important is that you do not give up on your dream.

Dreams are most successful when the intent of the dreamer is to experience joy. Notoriety and a large amount of money should not be your objective, because if this is your only intent, once you have arrived, you may not feel fulfilled. Following your dream is more about spending your days doing something you love, and finding the joy in the journey. When you do what you love, the money will eventually follow. Sometimes it is not always in your preferred time frame, but if you persevere, move through the obstacles you'll encounter, and continue to pursue your dream because you cannot imagine not pursuing it, you will get to your destination.

If you are a young person, do not let time slip away. Get started on your dreams today and do not look back. If you are an older person, it is never too late to follow your dreams. Be realistic about what it is you want to accomplish, and be grateful for those who were courageous enough to pursue their dreams in spite of major setbacks. Their examples show you that sometimes the only limitation you have is in your mind.

Our life experiences mold who we are as individuals. By the time I was eighteen, experience had already developed me into a very focused, driven, and career-oriented young woman. Without a formal education, I not only managed to secure a solid job at a large company, but I was also able to pursue a career that paid me extremely well.

The problem was that in spite of my career success, my marriage, and my first child, I felt something was missing. Was this what I imagined for myself and my life? Was this my dream? Marriage and children were never part of my dream. It was what was expected of me by my family and by society, and so, with resistance, I chose marriage and family. This choice caused others and me a great deal of unhappiness.

At the age of sixteen, I attended my first Broadway show in New York, and that is when I decided I wanted to be an entertainer. For the next fifteen years of my life I performed on local stages, primarily in musicals. With hard work I was able to progress from singing in the chorus to performing leading roles in shows such as *Guys & Dolls*, *Fiddler on the Roof*, and *The Sound of Music*. My love for theater continued long after I was married and my son was born. Today it is still one of my greatest loves.

I was thirty years old when I came to the conclusion that there were many people on television who were not very talented, so it occurred to me that if they could pursue an acting career, why couldn't I? At the time I came to this conclusion, I was very fortunate to be working a job in I.T. where I put in twelve hours a day, three days a week, which left me four days a week to do whatever I wanted to do. That is when it hit me. Why not use my time off to head into New York City, to study the craft?

My journey into the professional arena of acting was one of the most exciting times of my life and for a brief period of time, I found something that made me really happy. The first teacher I studied with was Gene Frankel, a director most well-known in the off-Broadway arena. His direction of the production *The Blacks* was regarded as a groundbreaking production in promoting African-American theatre during the civil-rights movement. It opened in 1961 and starred James Earl Jones, Roscoe Lee Browne, Louis Gossett, Jr., Cicely Tyson, and Maya Angelou. Frankel began as an actor himself and was a member of the Actor's Studio, which made its mark because of Lee Strasberg, who was best known for teaching method acting. In 1970, Gene directed Stacy Keach in Broadway's *Indians,* which earned him a Tony Award nomination for Best Play. Even though my interview with Gene was over 25 years ago, I can still remember it as clear as day. He grilled his incoming students until he was convinced that we did not have stardom in our eyes, because he only wanted to teach those who were focused on the craft rather than becoming famous. I was ecstatic at being accepted into his class. Although Gene is no longer with us, his school still exists today in New York City.

Several years after our first meeting Gene sat down with me to talk about my growth as an actor. He told me my greatest gift was comedic timing, something not all actors are blessed with, and that I could do both comedy and drama. I had never been able to cry during a scene until I studied with Gene Frankel. When I experienced those types of scenes in his class, my tears were not manufactured. They were an awesome byproduct of living in the moment. Gene felt I had what it took to be a success in the industry, and suggested my next step was to take a class working behind a camera.

Maria Greco was not only a teacher, but also a New York Casting Director. Maria echoed some of what Gene had already told me about my comedic timing. She also felt I was well-prepared for the "business" side of show business. In my opinion, and in the opinion of many agents and casting directors, not understanding the business of show business is what hurts many actors during their careers. Actors are creative types, and having solid business savvy does not always come naturally to them.

For the next few years I continued my studies until I felt prepared to begin auditioning. But not everyone was as supportive of my dream as Gene and Maria. My first husband, who tended to keep his feelings to himself, had a problem with my commitment to both my career and my dream, and turned to another woman to give him the attention he felt he was missing from me. This caused me to put all of my classes on hold as I maneuvered my way through what was one of the most painful times of my life, my first divorce. My son was only four years old at the time, so he needed to be my first priority. My dream was placed on the back burner. Fortunately, several years later, my second husband agreed to care for my son while I traveled back and forth to New York to resume my studies and auditions.

As excited as I was to be pursing this journey again, I continued to encounter a great deal of resistance from others. My friend and former high school acting teacher made fun of me and told me I was doing it backwards because I didn't pursue this when I was younger. As for my five sisters, I had one that supported me, and the rest of them thought I was crazy. My mother was frustrated with me because she wanted me to "settle down," which meant being content with being married and having children. My husband's family did not support me because they agreed with my mother, that as a wife and a parent, I should be at home taking care of my family. I was frustrated with everyone's viewpoint because I was also the breadwinner in the family. Isn't that why men don't cook, clean, or do laundry? Because they bring home the bacon? I was bringing home the bacon, enough to support all three of us, and at times even pay my husband's child support from his first marriage. Yet everyone still wanted to domesticate me because they didn't understand who I needed to be.

As I continued along my journey I was unaware that there were many insecurities bubbling underneath the surface of my husband's support. He chose to cope with his feelings of neglect by having an affair while I was performing in New York. He was fearful that I would fall in love with another actor or that I would move to Los Angeles without him one day. So, he gave me an ultimatum. It was either him or "showbiz." In trying to do the "right" thing for my family, my dream once again came to a screeching halt. My biggest regret in life was declining an invitation to audition for a pilot produced by Robert DeNiro's production company in New York, a project in which DeNiro himself would be directing. I cried for days after I declined that audition, and have lived with that regret since that day.

Several years later, at the age of 39, I unexpectedly became pregnant. Although my second marriage ended a year later, I was not able to return to acting because I was now a single parent again. My son and my daughter had to be my first priority.

But God works in mysterious ways. After moving to California in 2004, I became involved in a film documentary, which resurrected my life-long dream once again. While working full-time and attending college, I continued to dabble in the arts to prepare me for where I am at right now. My son is 30 years old, has a successful career in Washington D.C., and is engaged to be married. My daughter is 17, and is a little over one year away from leaving for college. Today, in Los Angeles, I continue to pursue my craft and the dream, because, simply put, it feeds my soul.

My point in relaying this story is that you must not let life pass you by. Do not let the naysayers hold you back from doing what you love. Do not let others define who you want to be. Do not accept ultimatums from anyone. Set your goals, honor your uniqueness and your gifts, and know that everyone has a purpose. Grab hold of your passions and do not let go of them—no matter what life has in store for you.

These Are My Dreams And Passions

What I Can Do Right Now To Pursue My Dream

9

Self-Reliance Is A Virtue

The strongest man in the world is he who stands most alone.
~Henrik Ibsen

Self-reliance is one of my favorite empowerment topics. To capture it in a nutshell: NO ONE IS RESPONSIBLE FOR YOU EXCEPT YOU!

Society has set a precedent that men are responsible for taking care of the women in their lives. Even in the new millennium, women continue to seek out men with money to marry. This is an archaic way of thinking, as women are now afforded the same opportunities to make large sums of money for themselves. If a woman ever desires to become fully empowered, she must stop relying on a man to take care of her. With the divorce rate being as high as it is, she puts herself at risk of being financially devastated should her marriage end. What if she is the one who has the desire to leave? What if she is in a painful, or even worse, an abusive relationship, and she has given up all of her power to leave because she relies on another individual to take care of her? I understand this may all sound negative to those who want to believe in happily ever after, but a friend of mine wrote an entire book on this topic to help empower other women who have lived through this life challenge. Unfortunately, this scenario is a reality for many. Whether you are a man or a woman, making the choice to allow another person to take care of you financially gives that other person all of the power in the relationship, and strips you of a very important piece of yourself.

If you are a young person living in your parents' home, the same concept applies. I recognize that times are challenging right now. Being alone and financially responsible for yourself can be frightening. Nevertheless, I still believe it is better to be on your own with four roommates than it is to live at home with your parents. As long as you choose to remain dependent on your parents, you will continue to be a child in many ways. The road to self-empowerment will disappear unless you venture out into the world on your own, and live your life according to your own rules and expectations, not the rules and expectations of others. Of course you will make mistakes. Of course you will stumble and fall. These are the ways in which you will learn and master self-reliance.

Becoming financially self-sufficient is not the only aspect of self-reliance to address. Let's talk about emotional self-reliance. There will be times in your life when you might have to go it alone. We all have little or no control over life, and what it may bring our way, whether it is the loss of a job, a pet, divorce, an ending of a friendship, or even the death of a loved one. When these events happen, you cannot fall apart because there is no one to pick you up. You have to be able to pick yourself up and move forward whether you have support from others or not. Mastering this aspect of your life makes you feel strong, liberated, and independent. It is wonderful to love others and to have their support. However, *needing* others to do what you should be able to do for yourself will always lead to loneliness, emotional despair, and disappointment in others and in life.

Many people say, "I don't want to die alone." Think about that statement for a minute. Doesn't everyone die alone? Are your loved ones accompanying you on the journey called death? Will they walk with you until you get to the other side? Rarely do people die in the arms of a loved one. Most times, we are alone when we die, or with strangers at a hospital if we are ill or are suffering from injuries from an accident. I think what most people mean by this statement is, "I don't want to die without feeling loved, treasured, appreciated, and valued." This is a feeling we can all have, whether we are in a romantic relationship or not. If you live your life loving others with an open heart, then you will never be alone, as these individuals will be in your heart at all times. Even if these very special people cannot be there for you physically at the time of your death, you will not feel alone when you pass. Your heart will be full and you will end your journey here with very little regret.

As you continue your journey of becoming more self-reliant, you may begin to realize why there are so many self-help and do-it-yourself books on the market. These publications teach people how to do things for themselves. Technology has also provided us with easily accessible how-to videos. Search any given topic on the Internet and you may find an answer to your problem.

I am not saying we should do away with professionals that are here to help us. They certainly have their place. Unless we are independently wealthy and can afford to employ others and help them by giving them an income, why spend our hard-earned money paying others to do what we can, in many cases, do for ourselves? Before you hire a professional, do a little research on your own. You may find out that not only can you do something for yourself, but you'll actually enjoy learning how to do it. Whether you are planning your own wedding, fixing a broken handle on your toilet, or filing for a divorce, take the time to do your homework and research what it is you want to accomplish prior to consulting a professional. This homework might also prevent you from being taken advantage of. Once you have achieved success in doing things for yourself, you will feel more confident to try the next unknown task alone. Nothing will make you feel more empowered and alive than achieving your own results.

This next topic may be a bit unsettling for some. Part of becoming self-reliant and self-empowered is taking your health into your own hands. Your emotional health, and how you manage it, has an impact on your physical health. Negative emotions are toxic to your body, and so are stress and anxiety. When you learn to take control of your emotions and your life, you will see some of your physical ailments disappear. If you need to go to a doctor to treat the illness, then by all means do so. In many cases, you will need the extra help of a physician or medication to get you back on the road of recovery. Unfortunately, many have lost their way and have come to rely too much on pharmaceuticals. It is important to get at the root cause of the illness, and work on that instead.

If you have read the works of Dr. Bernie Siegal, Dr. Deepak Chopra, Dr. Andrew Weil, or spiritual teacher Louise Hay, you will understand what I am referring to. Never underestimate the power of alternative, all-natural treatment, as well as your body's amazing power to heal itself. With the use of pharmaceuticals, sometimes the symptoms are treated rather than the cause. In many situations while one problem is treated, the side effects of these drugs create a new problem. Health care has become so expensive, and the quality of treatment has deteriorated due to recent insurance limitations. Doctors usher you in and out so quickly and provide you with less service for a higher amount of money. Keep these over-inflated expenses to a minimum by taking back control of this area of your life as much as possible. Learn as much as you can about alternative care that is good for your body. Eat well. Exercise. Meditate. Laugh. Relax. Love your body enough to take care of it and partake in as much preventative care as possible.

I used to be so dependent on others that I would call my sister or my son to hook up my DVD player or hang curtain rods for me. Not anymore. Not only do I do small things like this myself now, but I have also handled my own divorce, tiled my bathroom floor, successfully filed my own bankruptcy, taught myself how to do my own taxes for a small business, and a zillion other things I used to pay others to do for me. Even this book was *self*-published!

God bless the man who first taught me about emotional self-reliance. Ed Bergman was a spiritual teacher whose workshops I attended in Manhattan in the early 1990's. During one of our sessions he questioned me about what I do to feel better when I'm upset. I told him I seek out my husband to sooth me and support me. Ed instructed me that whenever I was upset I was not to allow my husband to hug me or comfort me. I was flabbergasted. Isn't that what my husband was there for—to comfort me during life's challenges? I thought this was the craziest concept when I was first exposed to it. In retrospect I see how powerful this lesson was and what a beautiful gift Ed gave to me.

Self-comfort takes practice because we are not accustomed to nurturing ourselves. Try to use the five senses to help you accomplish your goal. Take a long walk someplace where you can appreciate nature and all of its beauty. Go to an art museum alone. Sit in your garden if you have one and just breathe. Use meditation to cleanse your soul. Allow yourself to cry if you need to, and then take a hot shower or bubble bath to cleanse yourself of the negative energy you are releasing. Watch a movie that you love, or listen to soothing music as well as other sounds of nature. Bake some bread or cookies and take in all of the smells. Cook your favorite meal. Buy yourself some flowers. Cuddle with your dog, your cat, or your baby. Visualize a positive event coming into your life, or recall into your mind's eye a memory that makes you smile.

There is no one who can be a better friend to you than you. Once you begin to master nurturing yourself, you will quickly realize that although it is not a bad thing to allow others to comfort and support you, it is more important for you to learn how to do it for yourself. In the words of Ralph Waldo Emerson—"trust thyself."

Ways In Which I Am Self-Reliant

Ways In Which I Am Not Self-Reliant

10

I Gotta Be Me

I was once afraid of people saying, "Who does she think she is?"
Now I have the courage to stand and say, "This is who I am."
~Oprah Winfrey

Self-esteem is a major component of self-empowerment. How much we value ourselves contributes to every aspect of our lives. It definitely affects our relationships with others. It impacts our academics as well as our career success. When we value ourselves, we believe we deserve respect and love from others. When we do not value ourselves, we are constantly plagued by feelings of inadequacy. Poor self-esteem affects all of us, as it is at the root of many of the problems in our world today. It contributes to crime, abusive relationships, hatred, and addiction.

Our self-esteem forms fairly early in childhood and is molded by our personal experiences with our parents, siblings, peers, teachers, culture, and religion. As children, negative feedback from any of these sources may cause us to believe we are not valuable. However, as adults we have control over how we feel about ourselves. We have the ability to transform negative perceptions into positive ones, which results in becoming confident and secure individuals.

"Know thyself." This quote, spoken by Socrates, is one of the first steps in raising your self-esteem. When you truly know who you are, you will no longer feel the need to put on a façade or to be phony. You can just BE. To start, you must identify the misperceptions you have been fed by others. Then you must realize that these misperceptions are lies or untruths that you can acknowledge and then ignore.

Next you need to identify those things you like about yourself and those things you do not like about yourself. Identifying positive attributes about yourself will feed into your self-esteem. I am not referring only to physical attributes, but also emotional, intellectual, and personality attributes as well. Make a list and include all four elements. Physically, you may love your eyes or your lips or your thighs or your hips. Emotionally, you may like the fact that you cry during sad movies. Intellectually, you may be proud of your GPA in high school or college. With your personality, you may like that you are extroverted and have a great sense of humor.

After you identify the positive, you must identify the attributes you do not like about yourself. Physically, you may groan every time you see your love handles in the mirror. Emotionally, you may loathe the fact that you lash out in anger easily with very little provocation. Intellectually, you may feel ignorant when it comes to politics. With your personality, you may dislike that you're so critical of others or that you talk too much. Then you must make a conscious decision. Can you change those negative attributes? If you feel you can, then you must try.

Reality-testing is a cognitive process that can help you to shift how you feel about yourself. Select the first negative attribute from your list. For example, if you're feeling that you are ugly and undesirable, you need to look at the evidence to support that belief. Let's say that you have had three dates in the past month in which two have become second dates. This evidence supports the reality that you *are* desirable to others, not that you are ugly and undesirable.

If you are unable to change the attribute or the belief you hold about that attribute, or you do not have a strong desire to make a change, then you must move to a place of acceptance about those attributes. You must face the fact that you cannot always change everything you want to change, and that acceptance is one of the ways in which you can love yourself. You will not serve your self-esteem or use your energy wisely by beating yourself up for something that you cannot or will not change.

Another thing you must stop is comparing yourself to others. This is a useless method of self-assessment. Comparing yourself to others erodes your self-value, your self-confidence, and ultimately your self-esteem. Others are who they are, and you are who you are. You are unique, and this should be valued. You have strengths and weaknesses, and so do others. It is also important to acknowledge that no matter how good you are at something, there is probably going to be someone else who can do it even better. *You* may be that person to someone else as well. Since being the best is a matter of perception, no one is ever really the best at all.

One way to shift the negativity of comparison is, rather than comparing yourself to another individual, first acknowledge the gift or positive quality that you see in him or her and then, if you can, tell that person. This allows a dialog for the person to mirror back to you what he or she sees in you. Acknowledging the gifts of others will lift their spirit, and in turn will lift yours, even if they do not return the acknowledgement. Being kind and supportive is a positive attribute to be proud of.

The last thing you need to do for yourself is to toot your own horn. If you see a good movie, you tell people about it. If you experience a great restaurant, you tell people about it. Yet many are not comfortable telling others good things about themselves. Some may say talking about yourself is egotistical, and this can be true, at times. It is not what you say about yourself that is egotistical. It is the way in which you do so that makes the difference. Those who are more comfortable talking about and promoting themselves exude confidence, and therefore move ahead of those who are not comfortable with self-promotion. The key is honesty. While telling someone how good you are at A, B, and C, don't forget to counter it with honesty about not being good at D, E, and F. This will show you are human and that you do not think you are perfect or superior, but only that you know who you are. All of this translates to one thing—confidence.

I am not encouraging you to be arrogant or to brag. The root definition of arrogance means "claiming for oneself" which is empowering, but the definition has gone through a transition and its modern day definition relates more to announcing positive aspects about yourself in a way that indicates you feel superior to others. This is something many individuals feel the need to do, because underneath their façade they are very insecure. If the only way you can elevate yourself is to put others down, then this indicates that you may be extremely insecure and have very little self-esteem to begin with. Do not be afraid to talk about yourself and be proud of your accomplishments. On the flip side, refrain from bragging or boasting as this is always a turn-off to others.

The best part of raising your own self-esteem is once you learn to value yourself, you also begin to value others too, which creates positive experiences in your personal relationships with family, friends, and co-workers.

It is important to realize that no one is perfect, which includes you, and that is okay. It takes courage to look at yourself honestly and come to terms with not only your positive attributes, but also your negative attributes. This is a necessary part of the process in the journey of self-awareness and raising your self-esteem. Denial about your limitations, faults, or shortcomings is a detour that leads you nowhere.

Accepting yourself as you are today with all your imperfections is a critical component to empowerment. It allows you to live fully in the moment and it guides you in knowing where you want to make some changes. Every day you can choose who you want to be or who you want to become. With hard work and commitment, you can transform yourself to become the best you can be.

My journey in raising my own self-esteem has always related back to the men in my life. Because of the negative relationship with my Sicilian father, my "Daddy issues" caused me to attract men into my life who treated me with the same disrespect he did. I tolerated physical, verbal, and emotional abuse from many men in my life. Someone once asked me a very important question, "If you felt at a young age that you did not want to get married and have children, then why did you?" My response was, "Because my need to be loved and validated was a hunger so strong it overruled my need to be a free spirit." This hunger, combined with my low self-esteem, led to a great deal of pain and suffering.

Once I learned how to raise my self-esteem, I came to a place of no longer accepting any kind of abuse in my life from anyone, not just my romantic partners. I continue to be extremely conscientious about who I allow into my inner circle so as to maintain relationships with others who are loving, supportive, and positive. I have laid the groundwork for no drama, no abuse, and no disrespect in my life. I have learned to know who I am and who I want to be.

One of my lessons in self-acceptance was when I recognized that I am, and always have been, a very candid and direct individual. Chalk it up to being Sicilian I guess, but I no longer find this to be a negative trait, although others do. I like this quality about myself and have no intention of changing who I am in this regard. I know that if an individual cannot handle a relationship with direct honesty, then they are probably not going to be around for the long-term, which is fine with me. In fact, my experience has been that I attract those who appreciate this type of honesty.

Individuals without self-esteem do not have the courage to speak out, as they fear they will lose friends or family members. The person with self-esteem speaks out because they are willing to own their individual truth, even if they lose friends or family members. I take pride in my Sicilian-Italian roots, and therefore I refuse to wear a mask in life. I fully accept who I am today and every day. I invite you to join me in enjoying the freedom to be YOU!

My Positive Attributes

My Negative Attributes

Attributes I Intend To Change (And How I Plan To Do It)

Recipes For Me, Myself, and Others

11

Control Thyself

You gain power over another person in one of two ways;
by winning their heart or by breaking their spirit.
~Anonymous

THE BIGGEST MISCONCEPTION ABOUT SELF-EMPOWERMENT is that it has to do with controlling everything in our lives, including others. However, nothing could be further from the truth. We can only control one thing, and that is ourselves. We cannot *change* another human being nor can we *control* another human being. If we try, we will either exhaust ourselves or we will exhaust the relationship.

Taking control of your life means exactly what it says. If you don't like what another person is doing, the most you can do is express your discontent in the hope that the other person respects you enough to try to change. Beyond that, you do not have the right to intimidate, blackmail, punish, demand, or manipulate others to do what you want them to do. You must respect their right to make their own choices. From their choices you can make your own choices.

Setting expectations in any kind of relationship, especially unrealistic expectations, places a burden on the relationship and is probably the number one reason that relationships fail, especially marriages. One person did not meet the expectations of the other, so the other decides to walk away and try to find someone who will meet those expectations. The only problem with this course of action is the new person will probably not meet those expectations either, especially if they are unrealistic.

Parents try to control their kids (especially Sicilian parents like me). Kids try to control their parents. Wives try to control their husbands. Husbands try to control their wives. Everyone is trying to change or control others whether they are in relationship with them or not. Take a look at the religious climate right now, and what you'll see is an expanded view of the inability to accept others for who they are. This always creates divisiveness. With the exception of abusive or hurtful behavior, when you are able to come to a place of allowing others to just be who they are, life becomes less frustrating, your relationships improve, and you are able to find inner peace.

It is important to realize that no matter how weak someone else in your life may appear to be, sooner or later they will tire of being controlled. They will distance themselves emotionally, or depart from the relationship. Some may even end up hating you for trying to control them. If you spend half as much energy trying to change yourself, as you spend trying to change others, you might find the happiness you so desperately seek through others to begin with.

Do we need to guide our children? Of course we do. Do we need to communicate our feelings and our desires in a romantic relationship? Yes, we do. However, what we need to be cautious about is trying to take control where we are not entitled to control. The most loving thing you can do with a spouse, a parent, your children, and your friends, is to grant them free will, even if they are making bad choices (in your opinion). Some people learn better from making mistakes. As they work their way through a challenging experience, they may master a lesson that contributes to their own personal growth. What you must understand and accept is that it is their personal journey, not yours. You cannot control them, and you cannot control their journey either.

If people you are dealing with have addictions of some kind, trying to control their behavior will lead to nothing short of complete chaos in your own life. Being supportive in their time of need is one thing, but trying to control or change their addictive behavior will not only be exhausting, it will also be futile. This kind of personality needs professional help that you cannot provide. If an individual chooses recovery, then by all means, offer him or her love and support. If people choose to remain an addict, you can still love them, but you must respect and love yourself enough to walk away.

I understand this is not an easy behavior to change. It is natural to want to control the outcome of situations and circumstances in life. The serenity prayer was written and became popular for a reason: *"God grant me the serenity to accept the things I cannot change; courage to change the things I can; and the wisdom to know the difference."* This chapter is about the wisdom that is required in giving the respect to others that we also desire for ourselves.

Once others in your life make their decision, then you can make a decision for your own life. You may need to terminate the relationship if what they choose severely impacts your life in a negative way. With more subtle attempts to control others on a daily basis, you will need to practice the art of relinquishing control or finding the compromise between what you want and what the other individual wants in order to find inner peace, as well as harmony in the relationship.

There is no way to find happiness if you allow someone else to control you, whether it be your parents, siblings, boyfriend, girlfriend, or spouse. Being controlled feels like bondage or oppression, which creates an enormous amount of stress in your life. Those who want excessive control have serious issues under the surface that need to be addressed by a professional. This level of wanting to control every move you make often leads to domestic violence or child abuse, and these are very serious problems. If you are involved in a violent relationship, your energy must be directed towards getting out of that relationship and out of harm's way, especially if you have children. No exceptions!

Other types of control are less obvious. Others may try to manipulate or intimidate you. Many times they do so out of fear of losing you, but that does not make it okay. Whether they are withholding love or sex, or whether they are demanding you to do exactly what they tell you to do, it is this type of control you must take a closer look at to determine if staying in the relationship is what is best for you.

Control and manipulation are two reasons why I am not very comfortable with organized religion. My religious and philosophical studies educated me about why and how religion was first created and the fact that it was intertwined with politics and used as a tool to control the masses. Today, both Christian and Islamic extremists infiltrate politics in an attempt to control those who do not hold their beliefs. Scripture combined with guilt and fear is used to control rather than to teach, which undermines the free will God gave us to begin with.

My first husband did not have very much control in our relationship. I know, I know. That is not uncommon when there is a Sicilian woman in the mix. I was definitely the dominant force, unless he was drinking. During those times he would find liquid courage and shove me around or manhandle me. On more than one occasion our neighbors called the police to assure I was okay. I managed to control his physical abuse by controlling how much he drank. I eventually divorced him, but not because of the drinking or physical abuse. I divorced him because of the emotional abuse I suffered during his long-term affair with another woman. It wasn't until after the relationship ended that I realized I tried to control him in an abusive way myself. My method of control was verbal abuse. When I was angry or frustrated with him, I would condescendingly lash out using words to punish and humiliate him. For years he did not object to the way I treated him. This was probably because he was raised by a woman who not only controlled his every move, but was also very condescending to everyone around her, so this type of behavior seemed normal to him. Eventually he grew tired of this dynamic in our relationship, and found someone else who he felt treated him better. He is still married to her today. Lesson learned.

My second husband definitely was the controlling force in our relationship. Even though there was a Sicilian woman in the mix, he was Italian himself and thus overpowered me through physical and emotional abuse. I always minimized his physical abuse, and I would keep most of what occurred behind closed doors a secret to protect him, simply because he never actually beat me. One time he locked me in a closet so I couldn't leave the house. Other times he would throw things at me or grab me aggressively causing bruising. Once, while my son looked on, he threw me into a glass door that shattered and came crashing down all over me cutting him on the face. When I would try to leave the marriage he would threaten to kill me with his hunting rifle. It was nine years of pure hell, but it was through the experience of this marriage that I found my voice and became self-empowered. And that is a beautiful thing.

It is important to realize that jealousy, possessiveness, and control are NOT love. They are indications of insecurity at a deeper level. If you allow insecurity to dominate and take over your relationships, it can destroy them. This is why it is so important to have love of self as you enter into relationship with others, especially a romantic relationship. If you are the one trying to control, this clearly indicates that not only do you not love yourself, but you are not loving others the way they deserve to be loved either. If you are allowing yourself to be controlled, it is time to make some serious changes in your life. Respecting yourself and honoring yourself are of paramount importance to becoming self-empowered.

Ways In Which I Try To Control Others

Ways In Which I Am Being Controlled

12

To Feel Or Not To Feel

Our emotions can take us to God or they can take us to hell.
~Alan Cohen

Feelings are the language of the soul. They have a distinct purpose. They guide us in identifying whether an experience is joyful or painful. To deny our feelings means to deny who we are. Loving ourselves means listening and acknowledging all of our feelings, even when they are negative, because it is our soul's way of speaking to us.

We have all heard others say "You shouldn't feel that way" which is a statement I find to be not only insensitive, but intrusive. Who is anybody else to decide what you should or should not feel? Have others lived your life history? No they have not. Do they really know who you are on the inside and what may or may not affect you? No they do not. Part of becoming empowered is owning your feelings and not allowing others to tell you what to feel. Just as you have the right to control your life, you have the choice to feel whatever you want to feel. To allow others to dictate how you "should" feel is to give them your power, and this book is all about reclaiming your power.

Feelings are extremely important. They tell us about ourselves and also about our relationships with others. Feelings can help us to determine what is best for us and also guide us in defining boundaries with others. However, there is one caveat. Just as you do not have the right to control others' lives, you do not have the right to tell another how to feel. It goes both ways. Remember that.

Yes, you have the right to feel angry. Yes, you have the right to feel sad. Yes, you have the right to feel frustrated. What you do with these feelings can determine if you are using your inner dialog in a constructive or destructive manner. If you are engaging in resentment, hatred, or revenge, you will need to take a closer look at these feelings, so you can transform them to something more positive.

Acting upon your feelings in a negative way can destroy you or your relationships. Suppressed feelings cause depression. Negative emotions, whether suppressed or not, can cause very serious illnesses in your body because they are toxic. This is why it is in your best interest to take the time to clarify what you are feeling, why you are feeling what you are feeling, and then respond accordingly to bring about resolution. Once you are willing to do the work involved, you can move through your feelings more rapidly, which is beneficial for your physical, psychological, and spiritual well-being.

Unresolved feelings can destroy your relationships because you may over-react to something someone else does to you. To protect yourself, you push others away. When your emotions are out of control, others may not know how to react other than to retreat. How you *choose* to react to your feelings, whether negative or positive, will be reflected in the outcome of that particular experience.

A great number of self-help books address the subject of forgiveness. Forgiveness is not about the other person as much as it is about you. Holding on to anger and hatred is destructive to your body, your mind, and your soul. Forgiving another is one of the best ways to show love to yourself. It is truly not about them. It is about you. Knowing this is a great motivator in learning how to forgive others for their indiscretions.

Forgiveness does *not* mean you have to allow a destructive or abusive person back into your life. It simply means that you move through your anger and resentment, and make a conscious choice about how you will proceed going further. In some cases you may need to detach from someone emotionally so you can move forward with your own life in a positive way. Or it may mean drawing specific boundaries with an individual to prevent this type of problem from occurring again in the future. If neither of these work, you may have to make a decision to eliminate this person from your life altogether.

Another emotion that is extremely destructive is fear. This emotion can be immobilizing if you allow it to take control of you. What you have fabricated in your mind could be completely different than the actual outcome of any given scenario. This is one of the ways you may hold yourself back. To allow fear to seep into the crevices of your mind is limiting. To become more empowered you cannot allow fear to control you. The best way to combat fear is to walk through the worst-case scenario, and then come up with a detailed and specific plan to handle the outcome if it actually arises. An example would be making a decision to quit your job because you hate it. The fear would be you might not find another job or that what you want to do with your life won't work out the way you had hoped. In this case walk through in detail what would happen if you couldn't find another job or you don't make the money you expected being an entrepreneur. What would you do if you encountered the worst possible outcome? Looking at this closely and outlining a plan B will help you make the decision that is right for you at this time. This will help you to minimize the impact of the fear, and also allow you to move past it. Every time you embrace your fear you increase your confidence to deal with fear in the next situation.

Suppression of feelings not only causes depression, it is also at the root of most addictions. The addict uses a substance, whether it is alcohol, drugs, food, gambling, sex, or shopping, to cope with feelings that are uncomfortable or painful. In order for addicts to fully recover, they must deal with the pain or negative feelings they have suppressed. This is the only way in which an addict will heal completely.

When addressing negative feelings it is important to speak your truth with honesty, but also with kindness and a regard for the other person's feelings. Although it may feel good temporarily to participate in mud-slinging or name-calling, such behaviors will only result in the other person resenting you or, worse, hating you. This serves no one, and later on when your anger has subsided, you may regret your outbursts and even feel bad about yourself.

Seeking revenge is also something that might feel good temporarily, but you may also regret it later when your anger passes, especially if you want to maintain a relationship with the other individual. Maintaining a relationship with someone who has been the target of your vindictiveness may be challenging, to say the least. Revenge will never help you to feel good about yourself, either. Even if well-deserved, being mean to others, name-calling, or being vengeful or vindictive will create negative repercussions in your own life. Loving and forgiving others, even those with whom you are angry, are part of loving yourself. Maintaining your dignity during challenging emotions will contribute to maintaining your own self-worth. Again, it is not about them. It is about you!

I have been practicing forgiveness for a while now. The first person I had to learn to forgive was my father. As I said earlier in this book, it was not easy to work through our relationship because he passed away when I was sixteen years old. At the age of thirty I came to realize that the pain of this relationship was causing me an enormous number of problems. I was carrying the baggage from my relationship with my father into my current relationships, and it was extremely destructive. In 1988 I watched a movie entitled *Leap of*

Faith with Ann Archer, which was a true story of a woman named Debbie who was diagnosed with cancer. Debbie worked with Dr. Bernie Siegal to self-heal, and she eliminated the cancer in her body through diet, meditation, visualization, yoga, and acupuncture. This film changed my life. The anger and destructive emotions causing the cancer in Debbie were associated with the pain and anger she held towards her father. In one scene, Debbie goes to the cemetery where her father is buried and reads a letter of forgiveness to him. As I watched this scene I broke down sobbing because it was much like my own experience. I viewed the movie several more times and I copied the monologue down. Using it as a guideline, I wrote my own version of the letter. I took it to my father's gravesite just like Debbie did, and I read him the letter. I told my father I forgave him, and then I burned the letter. I wept for about a half an hour afterwards, and I could immediately feel the cathartic release in my inner being that my actions brought. I also used this monologue for auditions in New York. It was so powerful and personal to me, that by using it at my audition, I ended up booking a large supporting role in an off-off Broadway production.

That was my first lesson in the power of forgiveness, but certainly not my last. Most recently, I forgave someone for something she did to me over twenty-five years ago. I had forgotten what she had done to me, or at least I thought I had. I didn't give much thought to her or the situation, until she was forced back into my life through another family member. Every time I was forced to encounter her, my old feelings arose and I would become angry all over again. If feeling this anger wasn't bad enough, I also hated myself for the way I was allowing her to affect me. At times I wanted to *go all Sicilian on her,* but knew that if I did, the repercussions with other members of my family would be severe.

I had to come to own the fact that I was making myself miserable by responding to her behavior with negative emotions. This is why I made a conscious choice to put the past behind me and forgive her.

I used prayer as my tool, and eventually I was able to make contact with her in a peaceful manner. We exchanged several emails and came to terms with our past, put it behind us, and agreed to move forward in friendship. The day we made our agreement I felt like I could fly. A monkey was removed from my back, and I could now interact with her in a positive way. This allowed me to see who she was now, rather than who she was then, and I actually learned to like her.

Your feelings are there to serve as a compass that will lead you in the best direction during your journey. This is why it is important to listen to them, own them, analyze them, and resolve them as you continue to move forward in life. This is one of the best ways in which you can honor and love yourself.

Unresolved Feelings That Need Resolution

Individuals I Need To Forgive

13

Agape Love

Infantile love follows the principle: I love because I am loved.
Mature love follows the principle: I am loved because I love.
~Erich Fromm

During my seventeen years of studying with my spiritual guru, he would repeatedly say two phrases in his diligent effort to help me grow. The first was "Love and allow." The other was "Bless the being and the path he is on." Although these statements seem simplistic, they are extremely challenging to integrate into the realities of life. Let's begin with what they actually mean.

"Love and allow" means loving and allowing others to be who they need to be at any given moment in time. It means accepting others for who they are, and loving them anyway. In a previous chapter I stated that you cannot change anyone except yourself. If you cannot change another individual, what choice do you have other than walking away? The change has to come from within, as you learn how to accept others for who they are. This is called loving unconditionally, and it forces you to grow up emotionally. No more saying, "If you loved me you'd do this." It is not for you to decide how another person loves. It is only within your power to decide how you want to love. Making the choice to love unconditionally strengthens all of your personal relationships—including the relationship you have with yourself.

"Bless the being and the path they are on" is used in situations where you feel compelled to help others because they are making bad choices, or you have anger and resentment toward another individual for something you feel they did to you. Again, this speaks to acceptance rather than trying to control others. If you want to eliminate some of the self-inflicted drama in your life, you must respect the choices of others, even if you do not agree.

Here is a small example. Maybe your brother is texting while driving and you think he is being unwise and fear for his life. You have had emotionally charged arguments with him about this behavior, and as a result he no longer speaks to you. "Bless the being and the path he is on" translated means your brother is on a destructive path, and you must respect his choice. He may only learn the lesson of how self-destructive he is if he has an accident as a result of texting and driving. As challenging as it may be, you need to express the risk he is taking with love, and then let go of your need to control his choice in the matter. You need to end the arguments with him, hold him in your prayers, and honor the path he is on, no matter how much you disagree. Rather than allowing your disagreement with him to destroy your relationship, you can use acceptance and unconditional love to allow things to unfold, as they will.

Our best teachers of loving unconditionally are dogs and children. We can leave our dogs outside in the rain all day, or forget to feed them before we leave for work, but when we arrive home they are not angry with us. They are happy to see us and are ready to show us their love with no conditions attached. Younger children also love unconditionally. Have you ever witnessed a child's behavior during a divorce when the parents are trying so hard to poison their child's mind about the other parent? It rarely works. At a young age, children have not been emotionally jaded. They see love as something pure and simple. As they move into adolescence and early adulthood, their judgment of others sets in, followed by conditional love. Why can't we, as adults, see love the same way as dogs and small children? Why do we always equate love with someone behaving the way we want them to behave? This must change if we want long-term relationships that are healthy, strong, and go the duration.

Make no mistake. Loving unconditionally does not mean allowing others to do as they wish to you. If people are treating you poorly, and you accept that treatment, what do they learn from your acceptance? Nothing—except that they can repeat the behavior with you over and over again. If you draw boundaries around the relationship to avoid poor treatment, or if you terminate the relationship to avoid being mistreated, you send a clear message to others that their negative behavior is not acceptable. It does not mean you stop loving them. You have simply made the choice to love them from afar. This is how you can love yourself while in relationship with others.

So many times I have heard both men and women in abusive relationships say, "I stay because I love them," which is a tragic mistake. Sometimes individuals need love so badly that they are willing to stay in abusive relationships rather than be alone. Their fears outweigh common sense, and all rationality goes out the window as they excuse the abuse to justify staying in the relationship. It is an emotional need on their part, which is masquerading as love. Loving unconditionally does not mean you have to continue to be in a relationship with another individual who is abusing you. You can still love and forgive your abuser, but you may need to do it from a distance until the other individual chooses to love him or herself enough to seek help, and make a change. Then, and only then, should you consider returning to the relationship.

To a certain extent, we have already learned how to love unconditionally through our biological family. We are taught at a young age that we should love our mother and father and our sisters and brothers without condition. As I said before, loving unconditionally does not mean that we should remain in a relationship with someone who is mistreating, abusing, or disrespecting us, and this includes family. If you are part of a family structure that does not allow you to honor your own truth and be who you are, you may need to love family members from afar and allow them to be who they need to be. You must love yourself enough to let them go. This is one of the hardest lessons to integrate into your life, but the inner peace it brings makes it worthwhile.

My greatest lesson in learning how to love unconditionally came during my third long-term romantic relationship. One evening, while out dancing, I met a very interesting gentleman. He looked like a "bad boy" on the outside. But on the inside he was a highly evolved spiritual being who hid this side of himself from most people he knew, including his own family. This was because they were Portuguese immigrants and devout Catholics who would not have accepted this side of him. I entered into a relationship with him because of his spiritual side, and also in spite of his biggest self-proclaimed flaw, which was being commitment-phobic. Since I had no desire to re-marry, I felt he was the perfect match. We dated for two years, and despite the fact that we loved each other, I never once brought up marriage or a cohabitation arrangement. I honored who he was, a man who was extremely commitment phobic. I had come to accept that he had his house, and I had mine, and the fact that we weren't going to marry did not denounce our love for one another.

My son, at the time, was thinking about moving out on his own. The three of us were discussing this at dinner one evening, and out of the blue, my boyfriend said "Justin, I have a proposition for you. If your Mom lets me move in with her, I will rent you my house for $500 per month." My jaw dropped to the floor. What happened to the commitment-phobic man I was in relationship with? I can tell you what happened. Prior to our relationship, this man was with several women, who all demanded marriage from him. He would tell them he wasn't ready, and they would push to the point where he would buy them an engagement ring or make them promises so they would believe he would marry them, and get off his back. The truth of the matter was, he had no intention of following through with his promise. When they would finally come to this realization, they would terminate the relationship.

With our relationship, he encountered someone who loved him in spite of his fear of marriage. I held no expectations of marriage or commitment from him, and this allowed me to love him freely and unconditionally with no strings attached. In 2004 I sold my house and made plans to move to California, and he was to follow me several months later. About a month after I left he drove cross-country for a visit and to deliver my car. At that time he pleaded with me to come back to Massachusetts as he did not have the courage to make such a big move. "I would have been with you forever," he said through his tears, and I believed him. Why would anyone want to depart from a relationship where they were loved without conditions attached? As I had no desire to return to the east coast, our relationship ended, and he very quickly moved on to someone else. Although our relationship didn't work out in the end romantically, we continue to be friends based on the mutual unconditional love that we were both able to give to the other during our six years together.

The ironic part of the story is that this man is the one who helped me to learn how to love others unconditionally in the first place. When I would criticize or point out someone's flaws, he would say to me, "Everybody has kinks in their armor." And he was right. Everybody has flaws. Loving others unconditionally allows them the freedom to be whom they want or need to be. If you really want a relationship to go the distance, whether it is with a lover, a family member, or a friend, loving unconditionally is a key element that will get you there. No amount of coercion, emotional blackmail, guilt, or force will get you what you want. If it does get you what you want, I can assure you that it will only be temporary.

One thing you must keep in mind is that when you love others unconditionally first, you must not expect them to return this type of love. If you expect it in return, then you do not love them unconditionally to begin with. Allow them the opportunity to learn from your beautiful example.

Unconditional love is not just something to be bestowed upon others. It is also something we need to bestow upon ourselves. We all make mistakes. We are all imperfect, and we all have "kinks in our armor." We are loved unconditionally by our higher power, and this alone makes us worthy enough to love ourselves unconditionally. Mastering this lesson makes us better people, creates a ripple effect in our lives, and provides us with the power to forgive others and to accept everyone on the planet for who they need to be.

Loving unconditionally is a no-strings-attached love, which challenges us to love not only our enemies, but to love others without expectation of something in return. It is real love, true love, pure love, and in the words of the Greeks: *Agape*.

Ways In Which I Love Conditionally

Individuals I Need To Love And Allow

14

Constructive Criticism

A successful man is one who can lay a firm foundation with the bricks others have thrown at him.
~David Brinkley

Many times we make choices which do not allow us to be true to ourselves, simply because we fear what others will think. This is self-imposed bondage. Learning to not care what others think, as well as using criticism constructively, is key to becoming self-empowered. No matter who we are, no matter where we live, no matter what we do for a living, and no matter what choices we make, someone is going to have something negative to say about us. The more we care what others think of us, the more power we give to them, and the less power we have over our own lives.

Everyone is entitled to his or her perception, but this does not mean another's perception is necessarily based on truth, especially your truth. Knowing who you are at your core, and fully accepting yourself, will help you to build a strong foundation that will hold up under criticism from other people.

If someone criticized you for having green hair would you be upset? Probably not and here is why. Because you *know* for a fact you do not have green hair. If someone criticizes you for being cheap, and you know for a fact you are not cheap, then your reaction would be the same. This is another area where you can use reality-testing as a tool. If you are feeling defensive about a criticism you have received, look for the actual evidence to support what is being said about you. Is it, in fact, true? Or is it simply this other individual's perception of you?

Sometimes when criticism is upsetting, it may be because there was some truth to what this person is saying about you, even if it was just a shred of the truth. You must look within to make a determination. Was it just this one person who criticized you for this attribute, or have there been several?

It is helpful to use the rule of three to decide whether to ignore the feedback you receive from others, or use it constructively. If three or more individuals bring to your attention that you are selfish, you need to take a closer look at yourself. If you do not want to be seen as selfish, you may need to make a change. Or maybe you are not selfish, but certain things you have done resulted in a negative perception, so you may need to make a change in how you present yourself to others to avoid being misunderstood. You also have the choice to say, "I know I am selfish, and I am okay with it, because it serves me well in my life." Self-acceptance will assist you in remaining strong in who you are, in spite of the negative criticism.

There will also be situations where others transfer their projections of themselves onto you. They may actually be the ones who are selfish, and they criticize you because it is a quality they recognize in themselves and do not like. Additionally they may subconsciously refuse to see that this quality resides within them, so they project their dislike of it outwardly towards you. When you encounter this situation, you must simply ignore the critic.

We all have a certain investment in what others think – our bosses, our spouses, our family, and our friends. Everyone wants to feel loved and accepted. Imbalance, however, occurs when you allow what others have to say, to limit your life and who you are as an individual. In these situations you must become your own source of validation. Every time you seek approval from an outside source, you move further away from self-validation and self-empowerment. You must find the courage to trust what you think, what you see, what you feel, and who you are.

Some celebrities are great examples of such an imbalance. Many have become consumed with having their egos stroked. This is because underneath their mask they are insecure and desperately seek validation and love outside of themselves. Their craving for attention is sort of like an addiction, and like a drug addict, they will go to any lengths to obtain their fix. In some cases this craving for attention is also what fuels an addiction to a substance. Some celebrities use drugs or alcohol to numb the pain they feel from rejection, failure, unworthiness, or fear of losing their fame.

There are also celebrities on the opposite side of the spectrum. Those who were able to ignore the criticism, persevered, and as a result, they reached their destination. Taraji P. Henson was rejected at a performing arts school, but she did not allow this rejection to invalidate her talent or who she was as a person. Today, she is an award-winning actress. Walt Disney was fired by a newspaper editor because he supposedly lacked imagination. When Lucille Ball began studying to be an actress she was told by an instructor of a drama school to try another profession. Steven Spielberg was rejected by the University of Southern California School of Theater, Film and Television three times. Oprah Winfrey was fired from a television job because she was seen by someone as "unfit for television." Here is someone who had all of the odds stacked against her. She was a woman, she was black, and she was overweight. She made a choice to not buy into what others said about her, and instead believed in what she had to offer the world, and look how that turned out.

In previous chapters, we've talked about allowing others their feelings and allowing them to be who they need to be. This means allowing others their perceptions of you as well. We both look at a man. I think he is handsome. You see him as unattractive. Who's right? Who's wrong? It is important to realize that in these types of situations, there is no right or wrong. There is only each person's individual perception, preference, and choice. When you attach right or wrong to any individual or behavior, you attach judgment. As challenging as it is, you must work to not judge others, and you must also work to not allow the judgment of others to affect your own happiness.

Excessively caring what others think of you keeps you bound to mediocrity. You need to wake up every morning, remove the mask you wear, know who you are, and live your truth. Everyone is different and this is a beautiful thing. Your uniqueness should be celebrated, not judged. Self-validation is a key component to happiness.

My siblings were great teachers in learning how to deal with criticism. I was the youngest child of six and always felt like the alien of the family. I guess you could say I was the black sheep, not because I did anything bad to disgrace my family, but because I was different from everyone else. Other than my outspoken behavior, I was a good kid. I was an honor student in elementary, middle, and high school, and my extra-curricular activities were focused around music or theater. I started working at the age of fourteen, sometimes two and three jobs at a time, and have always been career driven. I have been an avid reader most of my life, and am self-educated in matters of business and politics. I have studied psychology and religion both formally and informally. I have been and continue to be passionate about my causes. I have been a spiritual seeker since 1987 and am now a spiritual teacher. Many of these things have caused criticism from my siblings as well as their children for one reason or another, especially my spiritual exploration, and my conscious decision to not fit into the mold of what Sicilians, Italians, Catholics or Christians expect of me.

When I was younger and less clear about who I was, my family's judgments caused me a great deal of pain. Learning how to self-validate has liberated me from remaining in the box they would have preferred I stay in. It has been my experience that those who have judged me the most, including my own family, have lived their own lives with the greatest amount of mediocrity. They have allowed religion to dominate who they are and whom they love because they have not been able to think for themselves. They have chosen to be racists because it is what they learned from society when they were young, and they cannot move past those early influences. They refuse to try anything new, and limit themselves simply because of something as minor as not wanting to drive on a highway. In over forty years, these individuals have not grown intellectually, emotionally, or spiritually. I have made a choice to live my life to its fullest, and this means learning, growing, and re-inventing who I am every single day. Because of my enthusiastic approach to self-development and self-improvement, judgment from others, even my own family, no longer causes me pain or suffering.

As Eleanor Roosevelt once said, "No one can make you feel inferior without your consent." This is very true. Allowing ourselves to be affected by the opinions of others is like clipping a bird's wings so it cannot fly. I don't know about you, but I prefer to fly.

Ways In Which I Have Been Criticized

Changes I May Need To Make To Alter Perceptions Of Me

15

The Road Less Traveled

I'm going to take the high road, because the low road is so crowded.
~Mia Farrow

Mia Farrow is right. The low road is overcrowded, especially in this day and age when there appears to be an abundance of negativity and hatred in the world. Social media propagates the lack of respect some people have for others by allowing them to hide behind a computer screen while they type out horrific words directed towards another human being, without the fear of retaliation. Although it is challenging to choose the high road when others are working so hard to push our buttons, we must learn that this path helps us to maintain our own inner peace.

A Course in Miracles is a spiritual self-study course which is designed to help its readers transform. One of my favorite lessons in this course asks, "Do you want to be right or do you want to be happy?" We all spend an enormous amount of time trying to prove we are right and others are wrong, but at what expense? Sometimes we pay with our own happiness. Happiness should always supersede being right. Remember, there is no wrong or right, only our choice or perception. You must choose your battles carefully, and make sure what you are fighting for is really worth losing your peace of mind, and in some cases, possibly losing your relationship with others. An example of this type of choice might be fighting against oppression or social injustice. Taking action against something you feel passionate about may be worth the temporary loss of inner peace as the benefit from your actions might be your contribution to positive and lasting change.

Another game-changer on the road to inner peace is to stop complaining about something you cannot change. It serves no purpose other than to exhaust yourself and annoy others around you. Complaining wastes energy that could be spent doing something else. I'm not saying an occasional gripe or a venting session should be eliminated, as sometimes that is what is needed to force your feelings up and out. I'm speaking more about individuals who spend a great majority of their time focused on the negative. We are all familiar with the energy vampire who can bring us down into the hole of darkness if we are not careful.

Let there be peace on Earth and let it begin with me. We've all heard that song before. Becoming a peacemaker is an important aspect of taking the high road. There will always be others who cut you off while driving down the road, or someone who lets the elevator door shut in your face. It is important to not give your power away to the adverse people you will encounter in life, because unfortunately, they exist everywhere. Ignoring them rather than confronting them is most times the best option.

When people close to you anger you by something they say or do, it is best to not confront them at that moment in time. Take a deep breath, turn a cheek, and walk away. If after you've calmed down, you still feel the need to address the issue with them, you can do so in a much calmer and more peaceful manner. To handle it any other way transfers your personal power to the offender. It is also important to recognize that you cannot be peaceful with someone who does not have or want inner peace themselves. These individuals are filled with anger, mistrust, or hatred, and trying to make peace with them is futile. Always extend the olive branch, but if it is unrequited, you may need to walk away knowing you at least tried.

Looking within and finding your compassionate side is yet another way you can take the high road. Maybe an individual who is confrontational or angry is going through something, or has previously been through something that has made him who he is today. Feeling compassion helps you to alleviate your judgment, dissipates your anger, and eases your frustration. With understanding comes patience.

At times you may need to think of others before yourself in order to keep the peace. Divorce is an excellent example, as it is an emotionally-charged experience that challenges everyone involved. If you have children, you must think of them first in every decision you make. It does not serve them when one parent tries to turn them against the other, nor does it benefit the children to be used as pawns in a game between two people whose aim is to win by hurting the other parent. The only winners in this situation are the attorneys who will fight over trivial details so they can build their own careers and bank accounts. Finding a mediator to navigate these tumultuous waters is a more peaceful alternative to the traditional exhausting path of divorce.

Laughter is an important element in life that can help keep you on the high road. Laugh at yourself more, as well as your unusual and sometimes entertaining life situations. Laughter helps to reduce pain and blood sugar levels. Laughter will improve your job performance. Laughter is a tool that can hold together your marriage. Laughter stimulates your brain and helps you to cope with life in a positive way.

My biggest lesson in trying to make peace with someone who was not open to making peace came through one of my siblings. At one time I was very close to this sibling. In spite of what statistics say about going into business with family, we decided to do it anyway.

This particular sister never graduated high school and spent most of her work life as a waitress. This was why she was most comfortable opening up a restaurant. Because she was older than I, my biggest concern was if she decided to retire, or worst case scenario, passed away, I would be left with a restaurant which I really had no desire to own or run. We talked for several months about it, and came to the conclusion that a video store would be the best business venture, and one we could both enjoy. My sister had no idea how to start an entrepreneurial venture of this magnitude, but I did. This was why she continued to work at her waitress job, and I left my full-time job as a systems analyst to spend the next year putting together the store for a very low cost of approximately $35,000.00. The money came from my brother-in-law's retirement fund. Although my contribution was not in actual dollars, I had spent an entire year without a salary so I could design and build the store from scratch. My time at that point in my career was worth well over $50,000.00.

When we opened the store we attracted over 2,000 customers within the first few weeks. It appeared we were well on our way to success. Then a tragic situation arose. My sister owed back taxes, so there was a lien on her house. She wanted to take some of the money we were making at the video store to pay off the debt. We had previously made an agreement that all profit for the first year would be rolled back into the business, so we could build it to become what it needed to be for both of us to be paid a decent salary. A heated argument about money ensued. My sister's solution was to ignore me, and write herself a check. I tried to reason with her and explain that in order for the business to succeed, we had to make decisions as partners, and neither one of us could do whatever we wanted whenever we wanted. The following day she showed up to the store before we opened, and she handed me a receipt that showed she had pulled all of the money out of our bank account. As she walked out the door she said, "You'll be hearing from my lawyer." This was when the legal battle began.

I was winning the battle because my attorney was sharper than hers, so she tried pulling out all the stops. My father-in-law owned the space we were renting, and she approached him to ask that I be removed from the lease so she could run the store alone. She felt that because she had invested the money the store was ultimately hers. My father-in-law did not want to contribute to hurting me, so he refused to comply with her request. Shortly after that, one of my customers, who had taken a personal liking to me, told my sister he would pay her the money she had invested, and would become my partner. She refused his offer and told him, "I will burn the place down before I let my sister have this store." She put her energy into being venomous, while I put my energy into protecting my investment of time into the store.

While all of this was happening, my husband's uncle was experiencing a challenging time in his life. He had lost his wife in a sudden car accident. There was a lawsuit after the accident, and he inherited a large sum of money. He was struggling emotionally and was turning to alcohol to soothe his pain. He suggested that he buy the store from my sister, without her knowing who he was, and then he would bring me in as a partner because I knew every aspect of making it run, something he felt he could not do without me. He was excited that this opportunity would give him something positive to focus on, so he could turn his life around. His plan worked, and my sister thought she had found her guardian angel. The only problem was that he was really *my* guardian angel. Don and I re-opened the store about a month later under a new name. When my sister found out who Don was, and that I was still involved in the store, she was furious. She could not see that her own bad choices are what caused her downfall.

When it was all over, my sister pronounced me dead, which is such an overly dramatic, stereotypical, Sicilian thing to do. She has only spoken to me once since then, which was when our mother passed away in 1995. The moment my mother was laid to rest, my sister once again renounced me as dead. Why she didn't just call on the Sicilian side of the family to provide me with a pair of cement shoes I do not know. In any event, another one of our sisters became ill with cancer. Right before she passed away, she told me that my estranged sister campaigned to turn her and all my other siblings against me. My sister who was ill wanted me to know that she loved me, and would never sever her relationship with me. Sadly she passed away a few weeks later.

In 2001, which was seven years after our legal battle, I extended an olive branch to my sister by writing her a letter asking for her forgiveness and sent her pictures of my daughter whom she had never met. She ignored the letter, confirmed to my siblings I was still dead to her, and went on with her life. Eighteen years after that initial fall-out she is still clinging to her hatred of me. I am now convinced she will take her bitterness to her grave. As for me, I forgave her for her part in the drama, which is why I was able to extend an olive branch to begin with. I still love her and at times, I do miss her presence in my life, but I honor her choice. My lesson was experiencing first-hand that you cannot be peaceful with anyone who isn't already peaceful within.

Taking the high road is just like forgiveness in that it benefits you more than the other individual. This road provides less drama and more inner peace. It will feed into your sense of integrity as well as your self-respect, which like everything else you've learned so far, contributes further to loving yourself.

Ways I Can Take The High Road

Those I Need To Make Peace With

16

Life Support

Too often we underestimate the power of a touch, a smile, a kind word, a listening ear, an honest compliment, or the smallest act of caring, all of which have the potential to turn a life around.
~Leo Buscaglia

When we think of life support, our minds visualize medical equipment or treatment that sustains our physical life through artificial means. When we are alive and physically healthy, another type of life support becomes necessary to sustain our emotional, psychological, and spiritual health in a positive way.

Many people continually allow others into their lives who are negative, disrespectful, and sometimes abusive towards them. Why? Because all human beings want to be loved and accepted, and many are afraid to be alone. If you are ever to become fully empowered, you must realize that being alone is better than allowing your spirit to be damaged. The good news is that you do not have to be alone. You simply have to surround yourself with the right people.

We all have an energy field around us or what I refer to as our sphere. Everything is energy, including people. If you allow negative people into your sphere, you are affected by their energy. Negative people downgrade your moods and can even affect your health. When you make a conscious decision to allow only positive, loving, supportive, and inspiring people into your sphere, it will upgrade your moods and health. You will feel more inspired, and you will spend less of your valuable time and energy trying to fix relationships and working out the drama, and more time and energy loving others. It is important to surround yourself with the people who will help you to reach your true potential, and those who love and accept you for who you are.

Finding the courage to recognize which individuals in your life are negative and deflate your sense of self is not easy. You must consciously make a choice to draw boundaries around negative relationships that drag you down, or you must choose to walk away from those relationships completely. There is a positive side to making this choice. As you purge the negative people in your sphere, you make room for positive replacements. It is my experience that as each negative door is closed, another door, a positive one, will open. This process will allow an individual to enter your life who is more aligned with who you are at the present time in your journey. Trust me when I say you will never be alone unless you choose to be. Refusing to accept negative energy, especially in the form of people, is one of the greatest ways in which you can love yourself.

Granted, some of these people are family, and you might not feel comfortable eliminating these individuals from your life completely. In an Italian-Sicilian family we are taught that blood is thicker than water. Family always comes first. I'm not sure that I agree with this philosophy, and my older sister's long-term grudge against me says she disagrees as well. So first let me say that there is no written rule that says you must be part of a family that is abusive or negative. If the goal is to become fully empowered, you have two choices. You can draw boundaries around these relationships, or you can eliminate them from your life. Drawing a boundary means you might choose to not share some of your life with these individuals. You might choose to not attend every function they may host. You might choose to not invite them to every function you may host. You can choose to not listen to them. You can choose to not participate in their drama. You can also choose to give people a second chance, but you must do so cautiously and in conjunction with pre-set boundaries until they prove themselves worthy of more.

Not only is it important to surround yourself with individuals who are loving and supportive, it is also important to return this love and support in the same way. You must also *be* the loving and supportive friend, family member, or co-worker. When you put out this kind of positive energy yourself, it transforms your relationships, even some of the negative ones. When you smile, others smile back. When you listen to and are there for others in their time of need, they are there for you in your time of need. When you compliment others and tell them how much you love and care about them, they respond in the same manner. If they don't, you might need to look deeper at the relationship to assess its true value in your life.

Social media has become very prominent in today's world, so this is an area we need to address as well. It is a great idea to meet new people in this way, but you may also subject yourself to more negative energy by doing so. This is why it is important to take certain steps to keep your online social sphere positive as well. Use caution when accepting new friends. You're not in high school anymore. You no longer need to have a large number of friends to prove your popularity. It is important to watch people and study them before you allow them to get too close. It is best to align yourself with those you are in sync with socially, intellectually, politically, and spiritually. Accept no substitutes. Just because you went to high school with someone does not mean you need to keep them in your online social circle now, especially if they haven't grown or changed much since high school, or do not resonate with who you are today. Those you do resonate with can lead you to a solid, positive relationship that you can enjoy on a deeper level.

It is entirely possible to meet someone new in this manner who you feel connected to, and thus can have a joyful relationship with. Social networking should be a positive experience that is fun and rewarding. If it causes you anxiety or frustration, the only way to address those feelings is to hide people, hide your posts from those people, or live your truth and delete them or block them, because the cost of having negative people around you is your own happiness.

Approximately ten years ago, one of my sisters attended a gathering at my home with several of my friends. As she watched the interaction between us, she couldn't help but notice how positive and loving all of my friends were. She said to me later, "You have the most beautiful friends. You are so lucky. I wish I had friends like yours." I told my sister my friendships had nothing to do with luck, and I explained using a concept she understood—you reap what you sow. I believe I am a supportive and loving friend to others, and this is why I attract such loving and supportive friends to me. Even though I am now living in California, 3,000 miles away from these individuals, the bonds of those friendships she witnessed still exist today. Since moving to California I have also developed new friendships that are just as loving and supportive. Some people are so close to me, they are like a second family.

It is understandable that purging toxic relationships can be frightening to you. However, cleaning up your energy field is critical to your own happiness. Italians love doing that spring and fall cleaning ritual. I still love this cleaning ritual for my home, but I also use it to clean my physical energy sphere, as well as my social networking sphere. It always feels good to purge the negative and open my life to more positive.

Just say no to negative people and negative relationships. Maybe this wonderful mantra from my spiritual guru will help when dealing with others you need to release: *Bless them and forget them*. By blessing others you release them to their own path, their own lessons, and their own karma, while simultaneously blessing yourself by not agreeing to be part of a something so negative.

The best approach is to treat your relationships like a garden. Sometimes you have to remove the weeds in order for the flowers to grow and bloom fully. Be bold and do not be afraid to weed your garden. You are worth it!

Weeds That Need Removing In My Garden

Boundaries I Need To Create

Recipes For Me, Myself, and God

17

Living In The Light Part 1: An Introduction

God made so many kinds of people.
Why would he allow only one way to serve him?
~Martin Buber

As an ordained minister, one question I am frequently asked is, "What is the difference between spirituality and religion?"

Religion is a set of beliefs, practices, and rituals that acknowledge a deity as the ruler of our universe. It is dogmatic in nature, which means a certain doctrine is accepted without evidence of any kind and is not doubted by its followers.

Spirituality is a set of beliefs created by following an inner path of connection with a higher power, which results in an individual truth. Its focus is on many of the same things as religion such as prayer, practicing compassion, forgiving others, being content in life, taking responsibility for one's actions, being harmonious with others, and loving unconditionally. It is based on a strong belief that everything and everyone in the universe is connected, and that we, as individuals, are part of one supreme power.

Both religion and spirituality have the same ultimate purpose, which is to create a moral code for us to live by so we, as a society, can live harmoniously with one another. We human beings have a tendency to turn to a higher power when we begin to question where we came from, why we are here, and what happens to us when we die. This also occurs during extreme life challenges to better understand why a devastating event is happening, or to ask for help with the problem before us.

Living in the light is very personal. If you resonate with a specific religion, then your preferred religion is what you should use to provide yourself with inspiration and hope in life. However, if a religion makes you feel guilty, ashamed, condemned, or oppressed, then it may be necessary to begin the journey of soul-searching to discover what religion does resonate with you, or choose a path of spirituality. The latter will allow you to connect with your higher power in the way that feels most comfortable to you. Some may even choose Atheism, and this is an empowering choice as well. However, if you choose to believe in God, it is important that your spiritual journey excite and uplift you rather than weigh you down.

Those who feel oppressed by organized religion, but still want to maintain a relationship with God, may want to choose spirituality because it is not limited by a specific doctrine, rigid beliefs, or rules that do not allow you to be who you are at the core. The other downside of religion is that it is man-made which makes it, just like humankind, at times, flawed. Religion has been and still is the cause of war between countries. It is extremely divisive and creates an atmosphere of competition as one group focuses their energy on proving they are right and everyone else is wrong. This type of limited philosophy sometimes causes its extreme followers to feel justified in hating, judging, and even killing others, which is never appropriate if done in the name of God.

Would an all-loving, all-knowing entity really care about whether we danced, or went trick-or-treating on Halloween, things that are discouraged and sometimes forbidden in some religions? Would a Supreme Being really care about who we love or marry even if our partner were of the same sex? Would a Supreme Being care if we married at all? I highly doubt it, and here is why. Marriage was also something created by man to protect a family's property, which took the form of cattle, land, or anything else of value at the time, including daughters and wives. Many do not realize its original intent was not the spiritual union it has become today. The philosophy that marriage is between a man and a woman has nothing to do with God or Jesus, but more to do with mankind's judgment of others.

It is also important to note that not every religion or church is guilty of this negativity. Many masters have walked this earth to teach us about ourselves and about loving one another. My personal favorites are Jesus and Buddha. My intention is not to negate the usefulness and higher purpose of religion, but to outline the ways in which it is different from spirituality. Each of us needs to soul-search to determine what feels right for us.

I do not know of any Italians or Sicilians that are not Catholic. This religion goes hand-in-hand with my ethnicity. So of course I was baptized and raised Catholic. My parents forced us to attend mass every Sunday whether we wanted to or not. When the doctors told my mother I wasn't going to make it because I was a premature baby born in the 1950's, my mother got on her knees and like any good Catholic prayed to the Blessed Mother (Jesus' Mother) and bargained with her: "If you save my baby, I will name her after you." My mother's prayers were answered and as a result I was named Mary, and became a follower of Catholicism myself until early adulthood. However, I baptized my son as a Methodist because this sect of Christianity felt more comfortable to me than Catholicism. Yet, I was still very disappointed with God in spite of the fact that I was married, had a beautiful baby boy, a decent place to live, and a high-paying job. I was angry with God for all of the injustices I witnessed in the world, especially those which seemed to be directed towards children. If we were all his children why was he allowing some of us to starve, be raped, or murdered? By the time I was thirty years old, I had made up my own mind that God did not exist and therefore Atheism was the only thing I could believe in anymore.

Then, one evening I experienced what is termed a "spiritual awakening." I was lying next to my husband asleep in bed. All of a sudden I was startled by what sounded like wings flapping in the darkness. I lay very still for fear a bat had gotten into our bedroom from the attic or outside. My husband remained asleep while the swooping continued and I remained frozen. All of a sudden, I saw a white dove, which glowed as it swooped swiftly by my head. I sat up and screamed and this is when my husband awoke. I couldn't breathe or talk at first, and then I burst into tears and said, "Okay, okay! I believe, I believe!" Although some might choose to think I was dreaming, I know I was not. I had a strong sense that someone or something was trying to prove to me that God existed. This was a moment that completely changed my life.

This awakening in 1987 was a turning point that inspired me to venture into a spiritual quest to determine who and what God really was. Being Catholic or Methodist wasn't working for me. I spent the next several months attending different churches but always leaving because they seemed to offer so little, yet expected so much in return in the form of monetary contributions. Religion did not resonate with who I was, or who I wanted to be, because all I could see was financial greed, control, and judgment.

Shortly after this awakening I watched the highly controversial film, *Out on a Limb,* which was Shirley MacLaine's personal journey of spiritual exploration. This film prompted me to begin a journey of exploration of my own. I studied metaphysics, which focuses on the realities that exist beyond the physical world and our immediate senses. This led me to a variety of mediums, some of which were extremely helpful, and others that were obvious scams in an effort to take advantage of vulnerable people. I read every book I could get my hands on about metaphysics and spirituality. This is partially what alienated me from my family. They were not able to understand or accept my research or my newly found beliefs.

In my travels, I found one spiritual teacher I truly admired, who I lovingly refer to as DK. No matter what subject he spoke about, or to whom he spoke, he always came from a place of positivity and love. I spent an extensive amount of time with him over the next several years and began to put into practice everything he taught me. My life began to transform, and every little thing that occurred took on a whole new meaning. Learning about concepts such as reincarnation and karma provided me with answers to why there was so much suffering in the world. DK, and a path of spirituality, offered me answers to many of my questions that religion was never able to provide.

Later in life, when I began working on my degree in Spiritual Psychology, I studied the history and fundamental core beliefs of many major religions. My biggest take-away was learning how religion began and what its purpose was. In addition to being created to control others, every single religion was founded by an ordinary human being who simply disagreed with a previously founded religion. Once I learned this, I questioned putting any value in religion at all. I still admire, love, and respect spiritual teachers like Jesus and Buddha, but I have difficulty with the absolutes associated with dogma. When I hear an individual regurgitate what the Bible, the Bhagavad Gita, or the Koran says, I remind myself of how that person's belief would change dramatically if he or she were born on the other side of the world.

It is important to recognize that every individual is unique both biologically and spiritually. Therefore, when you make a conscious choice to live in the light, whether through religion or spirituality, you make the decision to enrich your life experience. Living in the light is literally the most powerful way to exist. As you connect with a power greater than yourself, you tap into the true miracle of life.

Ways In Which I Can Live In The Light

18

Living In The Light Part 2: A Guide

Someday perhaps the inner light will shine forth from us, and then we'll need no other light.
~Johann Wolfgang von Goethe

Living in the light and connecting with our source requires conscious work on our part. Some of the chapters you have already read in this book speak to living in the light, especially if we are focused on loving ourselves and others. Here are a few more basic guidelines to help you along the way. If there are concepts in this chapter that do not resonate with you, or do not resonate with your religion of choice, then by all means ignore them. I write about these concepts in the hopes that I can open a few minds, or feed those that are already open, but also recognize that some may not be comfortable with the philosophies that I choose to teach. For the purposes of this chapter, and certainly not to offend or eliminate anyone, I will address our higher power as God.

PRAYER: Whether we choose a religious or a spiritual path, prayer is extremely important, as it is our way of talking to God.

To maximize its benefit, prayer should not be focused on selfish outcomes, but outcomes that are best for all concerned. An example might be praying to keep a relationship. That relationship may not be the best situation for you, or it might not be the best situation for the other person involved. Praying to God and asking for strength to endure the pain associated with the broken relationship, and healing of both hearts no matter what the outcome, would be the type of prayer I am referring to, recognizing that the outcome may not be reconciliation.

The loss of a job could result in something better if you are able to let go of trying to control the outcome, and trust that God will always do what is best for you, or what you are not able to do for yourself. In essence, a life challenge could turn out to be a blessing in disguise. It is also important to pray for others, which will bless both the giver and the receiver. Your ultimate challenge is to pray for someone you don't particularly like, or someone you are angry with. This type of prayer produces amazing results for you because it elevates your spiritual frequency and attracts positive changes in your life.

MEDITATION: Prayer is when we speak to God, and meditation is when we listen to God. Life can be very distracting, especially with today's technology clamoring for your attention. Taking time to be alone to connect with your source is critical to your spiritual growth and your inner peace. Meditation is not always sitting on a pillow and deep breathing with your eyes closed. It can take many forms, such as a walk in the woods or sitting near the ocean listening to the waves roll in. It can be walking around your neighborhood while listening to soothing music. Or a bubble bath with lit candles placed around you. Meditation is a tool you can use to look within for answers rather than looking to others for answers. Only you know what is in your heart, and only God knows what will serve you best. Meditation provides you with a connection to both your heart and God, and it also helps to cleanse you of negativity whether the source is from others or self-created. There are physical benefits as well, including reduction of stress, anxiety, worry, and depression, just to name a few. Practicing meditation charges your physical, emotional, and spiritual batteries.

Many people who have never meditated are intimidated by the process. Here is an exercise for the beginner who wants to experience what it feels like. Light a candle and sit in front of the candle with your eyes open. Stare at the flame and do not take your eyes off of it. While staring at the flame, begin to breath deeply and slowly, while gently removing all thoughts from your mind to focus only on the flame. Is it bright? Is it flickering? Is it beautiful? Is it colorful? Begin by practicing this exercise for five minutes and eventually work your way up to twenty minutes. If you feel the need to release during this process, which is sometimes in the form of tears, allow yourself to cry, which will cleanse your soul. When you have completed the exercise you should feel more centered, more relaxed, and more at peace.

INTUITION: One of the greatest gifts God has blessed us with is our intuition. This is yet another way in which God speaks to us. It is important to pay attention and trust your gut feelings. This internal communication guides you by either raising a red flag, or providing you with a feeling of knowing which confirms the path you are taking is the correct one. The best way to develop your intuition is meditation. Quieting your mind allows you to actively listen to your inner dialogue. You must also begin to trust your hunches and gut feelings. If something feels off, it probably is. We have all experienced discomfort in certain situations or when meeting new people, yet we do not know why we feel this way when it first occurs. Only in retrospect do we understand why we had the initial gut feeling, when, later on, the truth of an individual or situation reveals itself. Fine tuning this art form will help you to make better decisions in life, and will also allow an open channel for your own creativity and wisdom to come through.

THE GOLDEN RULE: *Do unto others as you would have them do unto you,* which simply means treat others as you would like to be treated. If we ever expect to evolve spiritually on a global scale, we must end the vicious cycle of hatred, intolerance, and judgment. It begins first with those closest to you and then, like ripples of water, extends to those you do not know. Don't wait for someone else to be the peacemaker. Become the peacemaker. Be the bigger and better person. Treating others poorly never results in feeling good about yourself. If someone else is behaving badly, be strong and do not become part of it. Witness it. Learn from it. At first you may feel like you've become a doormat, but if you continue to practice this behavior, you will soon understand that you are simply taking the high road and becoming the peacemaker. Jesus said, "If someone strikes you on the right cheek, turn to him the other also." This did not make him a doormat, but rather a loving and compassionate individual.

THE LAWS OF THE UNIVERSE: It is important to understand the Laws of the Universe. We have all heard this catch phrase: *What goes around comes around.* In the Christian Bible, Proverbs 14:14 says: *You reap what you sow.* These are both based on the principal of cause and effect. Christianity is not the only religion that indicates that when people do something bad to you, they will have something bad done back to them. Eastern philosophy calls this karma. The main point, however, is that it is not your job to decide how and when others are paid back, so never ever use this as a justification for revenge or vindictiveness. Instead you must allow the Universe to serve justice for you, so you do not create bad karma for yourself through negative cause and effect. It does not matter what other people have done to you. It is not in your best interest to judge them or punish them. Payback must be left to your creator.

If you come to fully understand how the Laws of the Universe work on a spiritual level, you can step away from being a victim. Whatever you are experiencing, you have created from past actions, even if you are not necessarily aware of it. You may become upset or devastated that someone hates you, but you must also realize somewhere along the way you probably extended this same feeling towards another individual, not necessarily the one who is directing this negativity towards you now. It is really very simple. Anger attracts anger. Forgiveness attracts forgiveness. Disrespect attracts disrespect. Respect attracts respect. Cruelty attracts cruelty. Kindness attracts kindness. Most important of all, hate attracts hate—and love attracts love.

This does not mean everything painful you experience is a result of cause and effect. Sometimes you experience discomfort because you have made bad choices. Other times it has to do with why you chose to come into this life. Many spiritual teachings indicate that we choose when we come into this life and already know ahead of time when we will depart. The real reason we are here, however, is to evolve. Those of us who have chosen to believe in a power higher than ourselves also believe we never die and that our soul lives on. Many religions and spiritual philosophies also promote the idea of reincarnation, which is the belief that after we die we make a choice to return to physical life in a new body to continue our journey of spiritual evolution. Accepting this as truth offers you the opportunity to be less fearful of death, and to be more proactive in being prepared on any given day to meet your maker. It also provides us with an understanding of how we may have attracted something negative in this life based on something negative that we may have done in a prior life. Unfortunately we, as human beings, learn best through pain and challenging life experiences. This means all negative experiences have a silver lining. It is your job to find out what the silver lining is.

SPIRITUAL GROWTH: Albert Einstein said, "Insanity is doing the same thing over and over again and expecting different results." This is so true, yet we don't see ourselves as insane when we make the same mistakes over and over again, especially with the same people or in the same situations. It is important to make a conscious effort to learn and grow. Spiritually speaking, stagnation is the equivalent of death. You must view your growth in the same way you view your education. Once you graduated from elementary school you moved on to middle school and the lessons became more complex. Once you graduated from middle school you moved on to high school and life became more challenging, yet more interesting and worthwhile.

Once you master a lesson, you do not have to repeat it again. In my opinion, spiritual mastery is equivalent to completing eight years of education to obtain a doctorate, although it may take a lifetime (or two or three) to complete your spiritual education. It is the ultimate state of being.

The wonderful part about spiritual growth is the magic that happens along the way. When the student is ready, the teacher appears. This teacher could be in the form of a real teacher, a book, or a film. It could be a friend, family member, or complete stranger. Through others you learn who you want or do not want to be. Every day you can reinvent yourself. This can be a very exciting process if you keep an open mind. As long as you are here on Earth, you will be learning.

BEING OF SERVICE: There is nothing that feeds your spirit more than being of service to others. Although the ultimate experience is finding a job that serves others, we do not all need careers of this nature to be of assistance to mankind. You can do so through financial contributions to organizations that serve others, or you can volunteer in those same organizations. If your neighbor lost her home because of a fire, you can make her a home cooked meal or you can start a webpage to help her rebuild. You can give as little or as much as you like. The most important element of service to others is your intent. If your intention is personal gain of some sort, then you are not being of service to others at all. You are simply manipulating others to selfishly gain something yourself. So when you give, give from the heart.

There are not enough pages to share my personal experience with all of these concepts so I will choose my two favorites to provide you with a better understanding.

I mentioned in a previous chapter about my sister moving to California and our purchasing a home together. I chose to ignore the gnawing feeling that I should not go forward with this plan. I was afraid that if I told my sister I had changed my mind, she would hate me. So I went through with our decision, and it turned into a complete disaster. That experience, as well as many others throughout my life, have taught me to acknowledge and trust that special voice within.

When I was a much younger woman, I didn't think I was doing anything wrong by dating married men. I was free and single, so I believed it was the men who were doing something wrong. This sort of spiritual ignorance is what I believe brought about a life experience where I married two different men who both cheated on me, ultimately causing the end of our marriage.

When I was married to my second husband, my car was stolen from the parking lot of my condo. When we reported it to the insurance company, we didn't have the money for the deductible, so we padded the claim and reported we had golf clubs in the trunk that we never owned. A year later, someone robbed our home and the exact amount of financial loss was roughly the same $1500 that we padded on that insurance claim. Coincidence? I think not.

There are a thousand other ways to live in the light, but all you really have to do is flip the switch and become a conscious participator. Once you open this spiritual door, you will find it hard to close it, even during the most challenging times of your life. If anything, it becomes the life preserver that keeps you afloat during your journey.

Ways In Which I Currently Live In The Light

Other Ways In Which I Can Live In The Light

19

The Not-So-Secret Secret

You create your own universe as you go along.
~Winston Churchill

Although it is challenging to believe, we create our own reality moment to moment. We do so through our choices, both good and bad, as well as through our minds, our emotions, and our hearts.

Many have heard about or read *The Secret*, the best-selling book by Rhonda Byrne. *The Secret* is based on the law of attraction and the power of positive thinking to create happiness. My only issue with this publication is that it is not a secret at all. Norman Vincent Peale wrote several books on positive thinking in the 1970's. The metaphysical concepts in *The Secret* have been written about and discussed throughout the New Age movement, which began in the early 1900's and gained momentum in the 1960's. I was first exposed to these concepts by my spiritual guru in the late 1980's. When I read the book, very little was new to me. What I do recognize, however, is that this author presented the concepts in such a way that they became acceptable to the mainstream, not only to the hard-core spiritualists seeking higher wisdom.

In previous chapters, I've touched on taking responsibility for our lives, living in the moment, following our dreams, loving others unconditionally, taking control of our feelings, taking the high road, cleaning up our energy field, loving ourselves, and the laws of the Universe, all of which are concepts of *The Secret.* The most important aspect of *The Secret* is recognizing and understanding that everything is energy, including people. Our thoughts, emotions, and words are extremely creative and carry a certain vibrational or magnetic frequency. It is through these vibrations that we attract into our lives what we want, and sometimes what we don't want. If we learn how to master our vibration, we can learn how to master what we attract into our lives.

If you are caught up in fear about something, what will you attract? You will attract the thing you fear most. If you think very little of yourself what will you attract? You will attract people who will reinforce your belief. If you obsess about your boss terminating your employment, what will you attract? A termination. In order to attract what you want, you must clean up your thoughts, your feelings, and your behaviors, which ultimately clean up your energy vibration allowing you to receive what you most want. In an earlier chapter, I spoke about forgiving others and how it serves you more than the person you are upset with. Here is why. If you are caught up in anger, despair, frustration, or hatred, you are lowering your vibration, so no matter how much you might think about or visualize something you want, you will not be able to receive it until your vibration is in alignment with what you desire to receive.

When you vibrate at a lower frequency, you are more apt to manifest disease in your life while others vibrating at a higher frequency manifest miracles. The average person blames or thanks God for these experiences, but God is only half of the energy that goes into creation. You are the other half. We all have a choice to believe in God's will, but this book is about self-empowerment, and part of the process is to realize that you are the co-pilot in all of what is created in your life. Remember, God helps those who help themselves. If your thoughts remain positive, you can speed up what you are trying to create. If they are negative, you will slow down what you are trying to create, or worse, manifest the opposite of what you want.

When you feel gratitude you attract more things for which to be grateful. Expressing gratitude, whether verbally or in writing, is a powerful exercise in creating positive life experiences. When you take control of your thoughts, your emotions, and your behavior, you essentially take control of your life. A positive vibration is always going to be more powerful than a negative one. You decide what will come into your experience, whether it is money, people, or the opportunity of a lifetime. Does visualization or creating a vision board really work? Yes, it does. However, you can visualize all you want, but if you are putting out negativity into the Universe, what you desire will take much longer to manifest.

One of the most challenging parts of self-creation is obsession. It is a common mistake when trying to create what you want, to obsess about how you are going to make your dreams come true. This is not necessary and in fact, only pushes what you want further away because obsessive thought is negative thought, and it slows the energy down. So you must not focus on *how* you will manifest, but *what* you will manifest. The "how" is the Universe's job. The "what" is your job. Things will unfold exactly as they should. All you have to do is keep your energy positive and take small steps towards your goal every day. You must also learn to accept where you are at prior to manifestation. If you resist where you presently are, and you feel depressed, angry, or negative, you are creating negative energy that pushes what you want further away. The concept seems simple enough, but it is not as easy to integrate into your life as one might think. It takes an enormous amount of commitment to bring things to fruition. Unfortunately, if it were as easy as creating a vision board, we all would have manifested what we wanted by now.

As noted in an earlier chapter, several years ago I was not in a good place. I was broken financially, emotionally, and psychologically. I walked away from my spiritual path because I was angry with God for leading me to California, only to destroy my life in every possible way. I was depressed because I had lost my home and was flat broke. There were days I called in to work and took a vacation day simply because I didn't have enough money to put gas in my tank. My sister, who felt I had abandoned her when I walked away from the house, would no longer speak to me. We worked in the same office and had to walk by each other's desks every day. It was painful.

If all of this wasn't enough, I was also experiencing the first symptoms of menopause and was acting like a complete nutcase. My son's former girlfriend pushed a few of my buttons, and I went all Sicilian on her in an email, which prompted her to show up at my son's job in tears. He was furious with me because he thought I had betrayed his trust in some way, but I had not. My son was never the type of child who disrespected me, so instead of picking up the phone and giving me a piece of his mind, or asking me what really happened, he simply chose to not deal with me at all. For eighteen very long months, he did not respond to my emails, my phone calls, or my texts. I would dream of him often and wake up sobbing night after night. My baby boy hated me. At one point, I even tried to justify his not contacting me by thinking that something was seriously wrong. Normally I would have hopped on a plane and showed up at his door to work things out with him, but being as broke as I was, this was not an option. A friend of mine worked in an investigations unit at an insurance company and offered to do a search on him. The goal was to assure me he wasn't dead or married to the woman who assisted me in creating this disruption in our relationship. I was relieved to learn he was still single, had moved to a new apartment, and his girlfriend had moved elsewhere. Although I knew he was safe, I was still saddened by the fact that we had no contact because of his refusal to forgive my transgression.

When I received *The Secret*, I watched it over and over. Life could not get any worse, so I made up my mind to consciously use this tool to improve my life. I made a list of what I wanted. At the top of the list was more money and less financial struggle, and a reconciliation with my sister and my son. Simply by creating a list and remaining positive, I began to see changes in my life. One day I was poking around on Craig's List to see if I could find a part-time job. This is when I came across postings for actors. I quickly realized this was a skill I could offer in return for payment. I went to Wal-Mart, had a cheap headshot made for under ten dollars, and started auditioning for gigs in the Bay Area. This is what led me to be part of a film that changed my life as it reignited my passion for this art form. I made a few dollars on other projects, and as my energy shifted further, I secured a part-time job teaching children acting every weekend at the rate of $25 an hour. All of this catapulted me out of my depression.

At the same time I took an active role in determining what I needed to do to officiate weddings on the weekends. Requirements vary from state to state, so performing weddings in California required research and investigation on my part. As a result of those efforts and again, a positive attitude, in my first full year officiating I made $8,000.00 for part-time work, and life became a whole lot easier. At the same time a miracle occurred at my job and in one instant, I was given an $8,000 raise, something that was unheard of at this time in the corporate world. I was witnessing a beautiful circle. The more positive life became, the more positive I felt, and the more positive I felt, the more positive life became.

On Thanksgiving that year, my phone rang and it was my son. He called to say "Happy Thanksgiving", caught me up on his life, which was going well, and asked me what I wanted for Christmas. I told him all I cared about was hearing from him. This was the best Christmas present I have ever received, but my son is very generous and sent me a new computer anyway. Finally, our relationship was restored, and I was ecstatic. Because positivity breeds positivity, shortly after this reunion, my sister invited me to her home and we resumed our relationship as well.

These are the reasons that I continue to utilize these tools in my life. There is one exercise I do which I have found to be extremely powerful and continues to change my life daily. Right before I go to sleep, I thank God for three things. Sometimes it is not always easy to find three things to be grateful for when you're going through a challenging period in your life. However, even saying thank you for negative experiences can create blessings in our lives. In addition, I also say three prayers. Sometimes I say them for myself, but more often I say them for other people who are in need. Again, to shift my own negative energy to positive, I also pray for people I do not like or people who have done me wrong. There is nothing that transforms your vibration more than thanking God for something negative, or praying for someone you don't even like. Once I am done with my thanks and prayers I visualize something I really want to create in my life. Not only is this a creative process, but ever since I began this practice, I rarely have insomnia. I always fall asleep while visualizing. I get a good night's rest all while sleeping with positive vibrations all around me.

All of what I have experienced has been living proof to me that if you work *The Secret, The Secret* will work for you.

Things I Want To Manifest

Things I Do To Lower My Vibration

Dessert

20

The End

Knowing others is intelligence; knowing yourself is true wisdom.
Mastering others is strength; mastering yourself is true power.
~Lao-Tzu

THIS IS ACTUALLY NOT THE end, but rather the beginning. It is the beginning of personal and life transformation for those who want it. Everyone can reach their full potential because everyone has the power to master their mind, their emotions, their finances, their relationships, and their health!

YOU HAVE THE POWER TO MASTER YOUR LIFE!

Changing ourselves creates change in others. This is how we can best contribute to global change. Grab hold of those destructive patterns and behaviors of the past which no longer serve you, and wake up every day and choose who you want to be!

This is a process. Be kind to yourself and do not berate or condemn yourself if at first you do not succeed. Practice makes perfect. Remember, it is progress, not perfection that is important. These types of changes are not accomplished overnight. They are gradual and continual changes which are created using a process that will make life more interesting and thus exciting!

What I can guarantee for you is this. The harder you work at evolving, the faster you will see results and monumental change in your life. Reading this book should provide you with an idea of where you need the most work. All you have to do is start the process! Once you have read through this entire book, take some time to go back to the sections that you find most challenging, reflect on them, and read them again with different eyes. Once you've had some time to put some of these concepts into practice, again take the time to reacquaint yourself with the contents of these pages to witness how much you've grown.

Somewhere in the midst of your journey, a light bulb will turn on and you will see everything from a different perspective. This will enable you to assess, analyze, process, and make decisions faster than you ever have before. You will be amazed at the results. Here's what you can expect if you are committed to doing the work:

- The freedom to be who you are and who you want to become
- Less anxiety and struggle and more inner peace and joy
- Less complexity and life drama and more simplicity and life contentment
- Less dependency on others and more dependency on self
- Less controlling of others and more self-control
- Less insecurity and more confidence
- Less compulsion and a release from addictions
- Deeper and more meaningful relationships

- ★ Unconditional love of self and of others
- ★ A healthier approach to your emotions
- ★ The confidence, perseverance, and inspiration to follow your dreams
- ★ A stronger connection to God, The Universe, or your Higher Power

I fully understand that internal change can be extremely daunting. If you need help, do not be afraid to seek it. Life Coaches can be found just about anywhere these days, and they can assist you in navigating the process.

Until we meet again, let me make you an offer you can't refuse. May the Universe make you strong in spirit, help you to discover your gifts, and encourage you to face each and every day with hope, love, and joy.

Namaste
(The Divine in me honors The Divine in you),

Sicilian Mamma

Reference Guide

Having a problem you need to reference? Use this handy guide to bring you back to the chapter or chapters that you need to re-read and apply in your life!